Feet of Clay

Democracy, Democratic Values & Destructive Influences

Bidemi Ologunde

DEDICATION

† Oluwabusayo Adepeju Ologunde †

(1992 – 2015)

CONTENTS

Acknowledgments   i

Preface   ii

1   Give & Take: Democratic Liberties   1

2   Nationalism: Political Ideology or Belief System?   10

3   Ideological Racism   21

4   True Feminism   30

5   Unconscious Biases   37

6   Growing Pains   43

7   Implicit Gender Biases   54

8   A History of Racial Criminalization   62

9   Threats to Democracy   70

10   Your Politics is not My Politics   75

11   Fascism: Where & When?   83

Sources   95

About the Author   104

FEET OF CLAY – BIDEMI OLOGUNDE

ACKNOWLEDGMENTS

My sincere gratitude goes to everyone I have had the opportunity to engage in conversations with regarding all kinds of social issues, some of which are presented in this book. Those conversations continue to catalyze constructive actions to improve our collective social, cultural, economic and political situations.

My immeasurable thanks go to my sweet wife (and editor-in-chief) Tobi and my adorable and jovial son Fola for their constant support during the long days and nights of the writing and editing process. I am so very grateful.

PREFACE

"Your Majesty looked, and there before you stood a large statue – an enormous, dazzling statue, awesome in appearance. The head of the statue was made of pure gold, its chest and arms of silver, its belly and thighs of bronze, its legs of iron, its feet partly of iron and partly of baked clay." –Daniel 2:31-33 (NIV)

A popular Yoruba saying goes: "what is not good enough needs prayers, and what is good also needs prayers." Historically, democracy has been promoted and upheld as the best and most efficient form of government. Wars have been fought and hundreds of thousands of people have died, all in the name of protecting and defending democratic values.

Despite these emphases on democratic principles, certain individuals throughout history, as well as in recent times, have taken advantage of democratic institutions and the collective social sentiments of the people, to create divisions, sow doubts and exploit weaknesses in society's fabric on their way to acquiring and consolidating power at any cost.

The social issues presented in this book are meant to further the conversations surrounding how best to protect democracy and democratic values from external destructive influences. These external influences are analogous to the statue described in the second chapter of the Bible's book of Daniel, whose feet of clay symbolized its own fundamental weaknesses. From its head downwards, the quality of the statue's construction materials gradually reduced.

Today's rampant social issues – racism, sexism, bigotry, intolerance, tribalism, etc. – all represent flaws and weaknesses in the fabric of democracy as we know it. Careful and deliberate conversations are necessary in order to carry out effective course-correction.

Before it is too late.

1
GIVE & TAKE: DEMOCRATIC LIBERTIES

Introduction

Throughout the course of history, democratic self-government was developed in order to end tyrannical rule. From ancient Greece to England, nearly every society has struggled with its share of tyrants. In fact, in the somewhat distant past, tyrannical and strong leaders were often viewed as an important tool for ensuring societal security and order.[1]

Gradually however, it became obvious that these leaders, who had either inherited or conquered their lands, often acted against the interests of their subjects. More and more people began realizing that the power of political authorities should have limits. The democratic process was designed to achieve this check on political powers, with the key component being the people electing their officials.

Yet, democracy did not solve everything. Democratically

---

[1] McGlew, James F. *Tyranny and political culture in ancient Greece.* Cornell University Press, 1996.

elected officials can threaten personal liberty, just as much as tyrants do. Those who fought for democracy thought that once the interests of political rulers and the people are identical, there would be no danger of tyranny. Not quite so.

Even when the government is elected democratically and acts responsibly, there is still a need to limit the power of society and government; democracy does not equate to self-governance, but governance over every individual by laws made by politicians who were elected by either a plurality or a majority.

This majority can easily become tyrannical and therefore threaten personal liberty via social tyranny, that is, the imposition of beliefs and ideals onto those who hold different views. Take for example, a situation where the majority adhere to a single religion. By using the democratic rule, the majority could use the force of the government to impose this belief on other religious minorities.

Clearly, democracy alone cannot guarantee personal liberty, but there are some steps that can be taken to avoid the dangers of social tyranny.

Rational Principles

If democratic societies want to protect liberty, then they will have to examine various aspects of their culture that cannot be understood without thinking about historical processes and human behavior.

The question of personal liberty should be addressed from a rational point of view. Yet, the rules and laws of a society as well as public opinion are influenced mainly by that society's likes and dislikes – in other words, they are entirely irrational. Furthermore, everyone in that society almost automatically assume that their collective customs are right and good.[2]

Consider, for example, how people follow the beliefs and

---

[2] Mouffe, Chantal, and Paul Holdengräber. "Radical democracy: modern or postmodern?." *Social Text* 21 (1989): 31-45.

customs of a particular religion without ever asking themselves why they do so. If a Muslim, who ideally should not eat pork, was raised in a Christian society, chances are she might have no problem eating pork. Ironically, she might abstain from all kinds of meat during the Christian fasting period of Lent.

As a result, modern civilizations have made little progress regarding the question of to what extent is social control justified, since the issue of personal liberty has never been considered from a rational perspective. The sole exception to this lack of progress is, strangely enough, the existence of religious tolerance in modern societies.[3] After centuries of conflict, religious groups on the European continent have simply had to accept that religious tolerance is necessary for stability, and that the individual should determine which religion she wants to follow.

Religious tolerance was however born out of necessity, not rational principle. As long as there are no clear principles that define when governments may legitimately exercise power over individuals, and we instead rely on our irrational feelings and the convictions of our social environment, there is no guarantee that our personal liberties will be protected. We must therefore identify a rational, more objective principle to guarantee our personal liberties.

Personal Liberties

What if someone you know is unconvinced that the powers of society and the government should have limits? What reasons could you provide to convince her otherwise?

Some philosophers such as John Locke have argued that ethical standards follow from natural or inborn rights.[4] Quite often, however, what we define as "natural" is very much subjective, based on the cultural whims of the societies in which

---

[3] Lacorne, Denis. *The limits of tolerance: Enlightenment values and religious fanaticism.* Columbia University Press, 2019.

[4] Locke, John. *Locke: Two treatises of government.* Cambridge University Press, 1967.

we belong.

In order to discuss the question rationally, we have to approach the concept of an ideal society based on the concept of utility: how beneficial is the law or other aspect of governmental rule to the well-being of humankind? In fact, only a society that respects personal liberties based on utility will flourish.[5] Without the freedom to make their own decisions as individuals, people will be unable to develop their own mental and moral capabilities, which will hurt their character and well-being.

However, personal liberty is not just important for the individual; it is also important for society as a whole. Only in a liberal society are people free to develop their own skills and ideas and realize their individuality. The diversity of individuality empowered by personal liberty has the potential to result in an environment in which people learn from each other and combine their strengths, thus helping all of humanity to further progress. Indeed, history has shown that societies that value diversity over conformity have a greater shot at flourishing in this world.[6]

The question therefore arises: should there be any limits on personal freedom?

Freedom of (Desired) Action

No one else is responsible for an individual's well-being other than the individual herself. As human beings, we have the capacity to come to our own judgments through careful reflection; ideally, people must decide on their own what to think and do, and no one should be allowed to exert their will on someone else's liberty.

One exception, however, is children. While adults have the mental capacity to make sound decisions, children, on the other hand, lack the mental and emotional maturity to do so. As a result, it is acceptable for adults to interfere with children's liberties, in

---

[5] Agarwal, Vidhi. "Privacy and data protection laws in India." *International Journal of Liability and Scientific Enquiry* 5, no. 3-4 (2012): 205-212.
[6] Gilbert, Alan, and Gilbert Alan. *Democratic individuality.* Cambridge University Press, 1990.

the children's best interests.[7]

Furthermore, society must not impose its beliefs and way of life onto all individuals. Unfortunately, members of a given society sometimes hold the view that it would be better for an individual's health or morality if they followed the particular religious ideas and moral norms of that society. These people often even feel offended by the way others live and act and might even want to prevent them from living this way.

For example, seventeenth century English Puritans wanted to forbid both public and private entertainment,[8] and because Islam prohibits eating pork,[9] some Muslims believe that nobody should be allowed to eat pork.

However, holding these views does not give someone the right to impose them on others. Individuals are well within their rights to attempt to convince others to adopt their beliefs, but society may not impose these beliefs with the force of law.

In summary, members of modern societies have the liberty to do what they want – in principle. This liberty, however, has some limits.

Interfering with an Individual's Liberty

There are some strong cases for limiting an individual's freedom in order to prevent harm. For example, society has the right to stop those who get drunk and then act violently, but drunkenness alone is not enough reason to revoke someone's liberties. It is certainly permissible to revoke the liberties of those who have shown a trend of acting violently under the influence of alcohol, for example, by imposing fines or jailing them. Due to their tendency to become violent when they are intoxicated, getting drunk in their case is a crime against others.

---

7 Tanenhaus, David S. "Between Dependency and Liberty: The Conundrum of
Children's Rights in the Gilded Age." *Law and History Review* 23, no. 2 (2005): 351-385.
8 Stannard, David E. *The Puritan way of death: A study in religion, culture, and social change.*
Vol. 573. Oxford University Press on Demand, 1979.
9 Shamsi, Rashid. "Why Islam forbids pork." *The Muslim World League Journal* (1999).

However, sometimes not doing things can harm the people around us, too. Consequently, society is justified to force individuals to do things that they might not want to do, such as make their fair contribution – in the form of taxes – to finance infrastructure projects like hospitals or roads. In addition, interference in personal liberty can be justified to save others from accidents. Although no one has the right to interfere with the liberty of individuals if no one is harmed, sometimes people are genuinely ignorant of the harm their actions might cause to others or themselves.

Specific & General Obligations

Not everything that might have negative consequences for others actually justifies interference. In fact, interference is only justified when somebody harms others by violating an obligation they have towards someone else or society in general. For example, although people are generally allowed to get drunk within permissible limits, it is clearly forbidden for on-duty police officers as they are responsible for the security of others.

Similarly, people have obligations towards their families. Although it is not society's job to stop people from drinking or gambling, when it leads to a situation in which people no longer care for their families, these vices can be considered punishable offenses.

Clearly, preventing harm is a complex issue. Some might suggest for instance, that because certain things will necessarily cause damage to individuals and societies, we have an obligation to prevent that harm. An example would be shops sell poisons that could cause harm or death under the wrong circumstances. However, because this is only potential harm, interference in our liberties is not justified. Not only are arguments in favor of preventing potential harm easily misused but allowing these liberties can lead to social benefits. For instance, shop owners who sell poisons can employ more people as long as they can sell those products, and those employees in turn use that money to stimulate the economy through societal obligations such as paying their taxes. If society is truly afraid of potential harm, such as poison abuse, then it can take other measures to prevent accidents, such as educating people on poisons or requiring purchasers of poison to submit personal data.

It is clear that what qualifies as harm and what measures should be taken against it are not as simple as they might first appear.

Freedom of Thought and Speech

Nowadays, there seems to be no question that freedom of thought and speech are protected and respected. However, many people have probably never thought deeply about why these liberties are so important to begin with.

Quite obviously, when it comes to their beliefs and convictions, people too easily follow the opinions of their social groups and accept the words of institutions, such as the church or political parties, as absolute truth.[10] However, neither we, nor the authorities to whom we defer our judgments, are infallible. In order to uncover truth, everyone must have the freedom to think freely and to express their opinions. Suppressing other people's freedom of thought and speech will inevitably suspend the discovery of truth, and therefore cause harm to humankind.

History offers many good examples of the suppression of ideas because they did not conform to popular societal beliefs. Even Socrates, one of the most important philosophers of all time, to whom humankind owes so many insights, was killed because people believed his ideas were dangerous.[11]

It is not only "true" opinions that need protection, however. Even if they are not 100 percent accurate, contrary opinions might contain enough truth to still be valuable to society. Sometimes,

---

[10] Aoki, Masahiko. "Institutions as cognitive media between strategic interactions and individual beliefs." *Journal of Economic Behavior & Organization* 79, no. 1-2 (2011): 20-34.
[11] Wilson, Emily R. *The death of Socrates.* Vol. 8. Harvard University Press, 2007.

opinions can add to the public discourse precisely because they are only partially true and discussing them further helps us get to the underlying truth.

For example, we now know that Newton's theories were not completely correct. However, if society had barred him from expressing his thoughts because his theories contradicted common knowledge, we would have lost many important insights that led to major scientific progress.

This therefore begs the question: what if someone's opinion is clearly wrong? Should they be granted the same liberties?

Allowing False Opinions

Most of us probably think that some opinions are just flat out wrong, and that people who hold those opinions would be better off just keeping their mouths shut. This is especially true for hot-button issues, such as abortion or gender equality. Would this actually be good for society? Short answer: no.

Incorrect opinions are valuable in that they force society to think about common, entrenched beliefs and reflect on why their opinions are correct. If a society wishes to commit itself to the pursuit of truth, then it is necessary that people be confronted with contrary opinions, otherwise they just blindly follow the beliefs of an authority or of the majority.

Regarding gender equality, for instance, it is not enough to accept gender equality simply because laws say so. We must also understand why equal rights are justified and why they are important. In this sense, whenever we are confronted by people who reject the notion of equal rights across the gender spectrum, we are forced to reflect on why our beliefs are justified and why great moments in women's rights are such important achievements.

Furthermore, if our common convictions are not continuously questioned, they will eventually be formally accepted and become ineffective. If we want to ensure that our most treasured convictions do not lose their power to affect our character, it is necessary for us to be continuously confronted with contrary opinions. Otherwise our various ethical and moral convictions become reduced to mere custom and we forget the underlying reasons.

Freedom of thought and speech are fundamental liberties that must be protected, no matter how questionable the thought or speech may seem sometimes.

Conclusion

The whims of culture and society are not objective enough to make democratic governance a strong protector of our personal liberties. Instead, societies must use rational principles in deciding which kinds of behaviors should be tolerated, in order for the individual and society to flourish.

2

NATIONALISM: POLITICAL IDEOLOGY OR BELIEF SYSTEM?

Introduction

In life, the only thing certain is death. As a matter of fact, two things have always weighed heavily on humans: the contingency of existence and the inescapability of mortality.[12] Attempts to make sense of both of them are at the heart of most traditional belief systems. Invariably, modern styles of thought remain silent on questions that cannot be settled by science, which is why neither liberals nor Marxists have much to say about immortality. Nationalists, however, do.

Take cenotaphs for instance, one of the most interesting emblems of nationalism. They are monuments dedicated to nameless soldiers, and it is this anonymity that gives these tombs their meaning. Because they commemorate "Unknown Soldiers" who lack an individual identity, they become symbols of

---

[12] Williamson, Timothy. "Necessary identity and necessary existence." In *Wittgenstein— Eine Neubewertung/Wittgenstein—Towards a Re-Evaluation*, pp. 168-175. JF Bergmann-Verlag, Munich, 1990.

something greater. They represent the ultimate sacrifice – dying for one's country. Cenotaphs seem to suggest that those who give up their lives for "something larger than themselves live forever.

In this instance, nationalism resembles religious worldviews. Faiths like Buddhism, Christianity, and Islam, for example, were able to survive for millennia in dozens of different societies because they tapped into human intuition.[13] These faiths bring hope that there must be a deeper meaning to the seemingly random ebb and flow of life. Whether they call it karma or the afterlife, religions find this meaning by linking the dead, the living, and the unborn into an eternal chain of death and regeneration.

Given this similarity between nationalism and religious thought, it is not surprising that nationalism emerged just as religion was faltering.[14] After being taken for granted for thousands of years, religion lost its self-evident believability in eighteenth-century Europe. This was the age of the Enlightenment, an intellectual movement that emphasized human reason rather than religious tradition.[15] However, the decline of religion certainly did not remove the suffering to which it had, in part, been a response.

In fact, this decline left a void at the heart of modern life. Without paradise, existence seemed unbearably arbitrary. Without the prospect of salvation and a life in the hereafter, the imagined community of the nation became more attractive.

The Sacred Languages

Imagine two strangers meeting in Mecca, Islam's holiest city, during the Hajj pilgrimage. One from southeast Asia, the other from northern Africa. They do not understand each other's mother tongue and they follow different cultural norms, but they

---

[13] Horst, Steven. "Notions of intuition in the cognitive science of religion." *The Monist* 96, no. 3 (2013): 377-398.

[14] Michel, Patrick, Adam Possamai, and Bryan S. Turner, eds. *Religions, nations, and transnationalism in multiple modernities.* New York: Palgrave Macmillan, 2017.

[15] Scherer, Matthew. "Secularism." *The Encyclopedia of Political Thought* (2014): 3368-3380.

think of one another as brothers. Why? Because they share one thing in common: Arabic, the sacred language of the Quran and all Muslims worldwide.

Religious and imperial languages such as the Quranic Arabic, Chinese, and Latin were defined by two features. First, they were written and read rather than spoken. In other words, they created communities of signs rather than communities of sounds. A similar example is how mathematical signs work. Thais and Romanians, for example, have different names for the "plus" sign in their respective languages, but they both recognize the same cross-shaped symbol.

Secondly, these three languages were truth languages. Learning them was not comparable to learning French for example. That is because the vernacular or "common languages" were not divinely inspired, unlike Latin or Quranic Arabic. They could not provide access to the true nature of things, which is why educated Europeans talked about turnip farming in German or Swedish but switched to Latin to discuss philosophy and theology. It is also why many Catholics were appalled at Luther's notion that the Bible could be translated into vernacular tongues. As they saw it, religious truths were not communicable in anything but privileged languages.

This view of the sacredness of certain languages, and their ability to provide access to the truth influenced the way empires and religious communities imagined membership. The Chinese empire's ruling class, for example, approved of the "barbarians" who slowly learned to paint the Middle Kingdom's signs – it meant they were becoming civilized. It was this mastery of truth languages that allowed Mongols to become Chinese, and Turkish nomads to become Muslims.

If anyone could be admitted into these religious communities and empires, there was no reason why these groups should not continue expanding indefinitely. Why then did religion seemingly fall into decline in the late Middle Ages? The answer was the effect of a concept known as *vernacularization* – the fragmentation of shared truth languages and their replacement by local languages.[16]

Print Capitalism & Language Consolidation

The invention of the printing press in the fifteenth century revolutionized communication. Books had previously been painstakingly hand-copied, and libraries counted themselves lucky to own a dozen volumes…until books became a mass commodity. By 1500, about 20 million books had been printed and between 1500 and 1600, roughly another 200 million more were printed. As the English philosopher Francis Bacon wrote at the end of this extraordinary century, printing had changed the "appearance and state of the world."[17]

Due to much of the printing of that time period being done by entrepreneurs, publishing turned out to be one of the earliest forms of capitalist enterprise to emerge in Europe and, like every form of capitalism, the trade was defined by a restless search for new markets.

When printing first took off, publishers primarily appealed to the continent's tiny section of Latin readers. That market was soon saturated though, which left the monolingual majority of the population who were non-Latin speakers. To appeal to them, you had to print books in languages they understood. And that was what publishers started doing.

Print capitalism eventually led to the vernacularization of print, and it overlapped with the Reformation period and the sixteenth-century movement for the reform of the Catholic Church. Before the advent of printing, Rome had effortlessly quashed heretical challengers by having a monopoly on all forms of communication. However, by the time Martin Luther published his theses in German in 1517, the monopoly situation

---

[16] Crossgrove, William. "The vernacularization of science, medicine, and technology in late Medieval Europe: broadening our perspectives." *Early Science and Medicine* 5, no. 1 (2000): 47-63.

[17] Eisenstein, Elizabeth L. "The advent of printing in current historical literature: notes and comments on an elusive transformation." *The American Historical Review* 75, no. 3 (1970): 727-743.

had changed. Thanks to print capitalism and the book trade, a mass market was in place for German-language texts by that time. Within 15 days, Luther's words had been seen in every part of the country.[18]

This was evidence of two things that had never existed before – a vernacular print language and a reading public situated between the illiterate masses and the tiny class of bilingual Latin readers. As this process was repeated across the European continent, print languages were standardized. Speakers of the huge number of idiosyncratic French, English, and Spanish languages who might not have understood each other in conversation, could now communicate with one another in print. At the same time, readers gradually became aware of the millions of people with whom they shared a language, as well as all those folks with whom they didn't. This was the first step to imagining a community on the basis of national characteristics.

The Newspaper Effect

The sacred languages Latin and Arabic allowed millions of believers around the world to form religious communities and feel connected to one another through their shared relationship with God. As previously mentioned, printing played a pivotal role in standardizing national languages, which allowed readers to begin seeing themselves as members of a secular community. It was not just the proliferation of printing that drove this process, in large part it was the particular format the printed work was presented in.

The German philosopher, Hegel, once remarked that newspapers were a substitute for morning prayers for the "modern man."[19] In many religions, the act of praying is typically a private act performed according to standard procedures. When

---

[18] Marshall, Peter. *1517: Martin Luther and the Invention of the Reformation.* Oxford University Press, 2017.
[19] Herzog, Lisa. *Inventing the market: Smith, Hegel, and political theory.* Oxford University Press, 2013.

the faithful pray, they are aware that the ceremony they are performing is simultaneously being replicated by millions of fellow believers. Even though they do not have the slightest notion of who these other believers are, they are still absolutely certain of their existence.

Reading a newspaper is a similar kind of "ceremony." Each morning, readers simultaneously open their papers and like believers at prayer, they know that millions of others are doing exactly the same thing at that very moment. The fact that these readers also observe folks opening identical newspapers when they take the subway or have their hair cut at the barbershop confirms that this imagined world is not simply fictitious.

The simultaneous act of reading therefore means that readers witness certain events through a shared national lens. Mexicans, for example, might learn of a coup in Argentina, but they do so through Mexican newspapers rather than through their Argentinian counterparts. If Mexican papers do not report on events in Buenos Aires, however, readers won't think that Argentina has somehow ceased to exist. Rather, they conclude that, like a character in a novel who disappears from view for a chapter or two, the South American country will reappear when its existence advances the plot.

Put differently, the way newspapers define "newsworthiness" creates a sense of a national interest. The reason Mexicans may not be reading about Argentina right now is because it is currently not relevant to Mexico.

This sense of a collective interest shared by otherwise anonymous readers of the same news in the same vernacular is at the heart of the imagined community of the nation. It is what allows, an American, who will never meet more than a handful of her 330 million compatriots, to be certain of the existence of 329,999,999 other Americans who, like her, are part of something called "the United States."

The European Linguistic Revolution

For centuries, Europe regarded itself as a singular continent. As the inheritors of the cultural and moral legacy of Christianity and ancient Greece, Europeans believed they had been divinely chosen. This meant Europe was not just a superior civilization – for a long time, Europeans thought theirs was the only civilization in the world. However, this triumphalist world view did not survive the European "discovery" of the Americas.

After coming into contact with other civilizations in the 1500s, Europeans became more interested in studying languages. This was initially born out of necessity – after all, sailors and merchants needed to communicate with the people they encountered on their voyages.

Over time, however, the study of ancient languages like Sanskrit and Egyptian hieroglyphics led to a couple of startling discoveries. Not only was antiquity more diverse, but many civilizations were much older than the Greek and Jewish worlds on which Europe's culture had drawn. In a pluralistic world, folks concluded, Europe was simply one of many civilizations and not necessarily the best one.

This discovery kickstarted the first scientific subject that regarded evolution as its core – philology, the comparative study of linguistic developments.[20] The philological revolution that followed led to the demise of sacred languages such as Latin, Greek, and Hebrew. These languages had previously claimed to be uniquely ancient and divinely inspired, but once that notion was debunked, they mingled as equals with their rivals, the plebeian vernaculars.

This then begged the question: if all languages shared a common, worldly status, weren't they all equally worthy of study and admiration? For Europeans in the nineteenth century, the answer was a resounding yes. This marked the beginning of the

---

[20] Errington, Joseph. *Linguistics in a colonial world: A story of language, meaning, and power.* John Wiley & Sons, 2007.

lexicographic revolution as philologists and grammarians started compiling vernacular dictionaries as well as collections of folklore and literary histories. The longer it took scholars to look at these vernacular languages, the more convinced they became that their speakers formed unique communities. This discovery was the basis upon which nationalist organizations argued for independence.

The first Ukrainian grammar, for example, appeared in 1819. Within ten years, Ukrainian had been molded into a modern literary language by poet and folklorist Taras Shevchenko.[21] In 1846, the first Ukrainian nationalist organization was founded in Kyiv, and in 1847, Shevchenko was politically convicted for writing in the Ukrainian language, promoting the independence of Ukraine and ridiculing members of the Russian Imperial House.

From Oslo, Norway, where the first Norwegian dictionary was printed in 1850, to Beirut, Lebanon, where American-educated Christians standardized modern Arabic in the 1860s and 1870s, this pattern was repeated. The systematization of vernaculars was not just a way of envisaging the national community – it was a way of bringing it into being.

Nationalism and the Logic of Imperial Rule

Nineteenth-century Europe was an assortment of multinational empires.[22] The Habsburgs in Vienna, for example, controlled a vast territory stretching from the Alps to the Carpathians that contained Hungarians, Germans, Croats, Slovaks, Italians, and Czechs. The French-speaking Romanovs in Saint Petersburg controlled an even larger empire that contained Russians, Tartars, Letts, Armenians and Finns.

As mentioned earlier, the philological revolutionaries going on in Europe at that time presented these empires with a serious

---

[21] Skurativskyi, Vadym. "Mystagogue of national identification. From the notes about ethnology by Taras Shevchenko." *Філософська Думка* 1 (2014): 8-23.
[22] Nugent, Walter. "Frontiers and empires in the late nineteenth century." *The Western Historical Quarterly* 20, no. 4 (1989): 393-408.

dilemma. Take for instance the Habsburgs. In the 1780s, the Holy Roman Emperor Joseph II decided to take the pragmatic step of switching the state language from Latin to German. Unlike Latin, German was a modern tongue already spoken by many Austro-Hungarian subjects with a vast literature at its disposal. That made it a solid candidate to unify the empire.[23]

But that was not how nationalists saw it at the time. The more the Habsburgs pushed for the German language, the more Croats, Hungarians, Czechs, and others felt that the state was aligning itself with the interests of one minority and ignoring their own interests. Reversing course was not an option either. If, for example, the Habsburgs decided to switch to Hungarian, they would simply create another group of offended nationalities that now included German-speakers.

Some empires attempted to break this bind by creating an official, top-down hierarchical nationalism associated with the largest ethnic group. This was then imposed on minorities, who were the champions of a more populist, bottom-up, nationalism. This is what the Russian empire did in the late nineteenth century when it introduced Russification, a policy that banned minority languages and made Russian the language of state, culture, and public life. It was a dead-end, and massive unrest and a series of open rebellions followed.

It is not surprising that this topic became so problematic for empires. The idea at the heart of nationalism was that nations should be ruled by folks who looked and talked like them, and this ran directly counter to the logic of multinational empires.

African and Asian Independence Movements

The First World War killed off Europe's multinational empires. By 1922, the Austro-Hungarian, Russian, and Ottoman empires were gone. On the continent, they were replaced by newly

---

23 Evans, Robert JW. "Joseph II and nationality in the Habsburg lands." In *Enlightened Absolutism*, pp. 209-219. Palgrave, London, 1990.

independent nations. The League of Nations, an organization that regarded such nations as the new international norm, took charge of diplomatic relations that were previously handled by imperial bureaucracies. Naturally, this question then came up: what would happen to the European empires' colonies in Asia and Africa during this new age of nationalism?

Three factors helped Asians and Africans in the colonial world to envision their future nations.

Firstly, it was technology. From 1850 to the early twentieth century, transportation and communication improved drastically. Telegraph cables allowed ideas to travel from metropoles to remote outposts in an instant, and new steamships and railways led to an unprecedented increase in physical mobility. This, in turn, allowed Asians and Africans to make colonial pilgrimages from their colonies to the imperial capitals in Europe. There, they picked up revolutionary political ideas, met their counterparts from other colonies, and learned about European struggles for national independence.[24]

Secondly, the education systems in colonies were often highly centralized. In the Dutch East Indies, for example, students from thousands of unrelated islands received identical instructions from identical textbooks. As they progressed through the system, they were funneled into an ever-smaller number of schools until they reached one of two cities that hosted universities – Batavia, (today's Jakarta), and Bandung, both in Indonesia. This experience consolidated an idea in these young Indonesians' minds that the archipelago in which they lived was a single, unified territory, however diverse its inhabitants.[25]

Finally, European racism reinforced the idea that colonial subjects in a particular territory were compatriots. Because colonial officials rarely bothered to distinguish between different

---

[24] Falola, Toyin, and Emily Brownell, eds. *Landscape, environment and technology in colonial and postcolonial Africa.* Vol. 6. Routledge, 2013.

[25] Kalidjernih, Freddy K. "Post-Colonial Citizenship Education: A critical study of the production and reproduction of the Indonesian civic ideal." PhD diss., University of Tasmania, 2005.

Indian or Indonesian groups, and instead treated everyone as despised "natives," these subjects often came to see themselves as members of a collective called "India" or "Indonesia."[26]

Together, these factors produced a new class – the bilingual, Western-educated cognoscenti. Its members were well-versed in the history of European nationalism and had experienced the colony as a coherent territory inhabited by people who shared fundamental traits. It was this class that would lead several different nations such as Nigeria, Angola, Portugal, Egypt, and Vietnam to independence between the Second World War and the 1970s.

Conclusion

Nationalism pictures nations as limited communities made up of people who share the same interests and traits, and above all, language. It is not a political ideology, however – it is more of a cultural system similar to religious beliefs, offering a sense of continuity in a contingent world. Nationalism was initially a consequence of "print capitalism." As booksellers sought new markets, they abandoned sacred languages like Latin and used vernaculars like German. This allowed groups of readers to envision communities with shared interests in specific territories. The standardization of vernacular languages and the emergence of newspapers then cemented this sense of collective national interests, eventually undermining multinational empires in Europe and in the wider world.

---

[26] Brah, Aviar. "Difference, diversity, differentiation." *International Review of Sociology* 2, no. 2 (1991): 53-71.

3

IDEOLOGICAL RACISM

The ideas presented in this chapter do not attempt to categorize every white/Caucasian person as behaving in a particular way towards non-whites/non-Caucasians.

Race: A Social Construct

In the United States, race has historically served the function of resolving a contradiction at the heart of the country's foundation. On paper, the creation of the United States was inspired by an ideal of equality between people. In reality however, it was built on extreme inequalities — one of which was between the slave-owning people of European descent (European Americans) and the enslaved people of African descent (African Americans).

Originally, the term "white" only applied to certain ethnic groups from Europe. For instance, in the early nineteenth century, Irish and Italian Americans were excluded from this category. It took time for them and other new groups of European immigrants to be seen as white. First, they had to assimilate to white American culture.[27] For example, they had to learn English and leave their old languages behind. As they assimilated, the definition of "white" expanded to encompass them.

The American legal system also helped to shape this definition. In the early twentieth century, U.S. courts ruled that Armenians should be reclassified as white,[28] while Japanese people should remain outside of the designation.[29] U.S. law itself codified whiteness into a form of privileged legal status. By law, white people were entitled to certain rights. Before the abolishment of slavery in the U.S. in 1865, those rights included the right to own slaves; afterward, they still encompassed most of the rights of citizenship, including the right to vote. In contrast, people classified as black were not allowed to assimilate into mainstream culture or enjoy the same rights as those classified as white.[30] Before 1865, they could be enslaved; afterwards, they could not vote.

As of mid-2018, white people constituted 100 percent of the ten richest Americans, 90 percent of the U.S. Congress, 96 percent of U.S. state governors, 100 percent of the top U.S. military advisers, 84 percent of full-time university professors and 90 to 95 percent of the people who decide which television shows, music albums and books get produced and published.

Racism vs. Racial Prejudice

To say that you are racially prejudiced against another person means that you *prejudge* her on the basis of the racial group to which she belongs. If you then act on your prejudice against the person, you are discriminating against her. This could take the form of ignoring, excluding, avoiding, ridiculing, threatening or

---

[27] Wildsmith, Elizabeth, Myron P. Gutmann, and Brian Gratton. "Assimilation and intermarriage for US immigrant groups, 1880–1990." *The History of the Family* 8, no. 4 (2003): 563-584.

[28] Lopez, Ian Haney. *White by law: The legal construction of race.* Vol. 21. NYU Press, 1997.

[29] Montero, Darrel. *Japanese Americans: Changing patterns of ethnic affiliation over three generations.* Routledge, 2019.

[30] Tatum, Beverly Daniel. *Assimilation blues: Black families in a White community.* Greenwood Press, 1987.

even committing violence against the person against whom you're discriminating.

In these senses of the terms, a person from any racial group can be racially prejudiced and can racially discriminate against a person from any other racial group. White people can do so against black people — and vice versa. However, racial prejudice and discrimination only become racism when one racial group has more power than another group and uses that power against its members in a systemic manner. To do that, the more powerful group incorporates their prejudices into society's laws, institutions, policies and norms, which they can then use to discriminate against the less powerful group on a group-to-group, rather than just an individual-to-individual level.

Thus, black people can be prejudiced and discriminate against white people — but they cannot be racist against them, because of the inherent imbalance in power between the two groups. For example, a black real estate agent could avoid doing business with a white person because of her race, just as a white real estate agent could do to a black person. But black people cannot create and implement policies that lead to white people being prohibited from purchasing homes in predominantly black neighborhoods, whereas white people can and have done so to black people.

White Fragility

Two significant developments helped give rise to the misunderstandings and denials of racism that underlie white fragility. The first was the civil rights movement of the 1950s and 1960s, when black activists and their white allies fought for black people to have equal rights in American society. In the South, they were met with violent repression from self-identified white supremacists, who openly espoused the racist belief that white people were superior to black people and deserved to have more power than them.[31] Newspaper photos and television news footage showed these white supremacists beating up black activists for sitting at whites-only lunch counters, attacking black protesters with police dogs and firebombing black people's churches. Many white people were horrified by these images, and they came to associate them with the word "racism." Under this association, a white person was racist if he acted toward black people in the openly hateful and violent manner of a Southern white supremacist.

The second development was one of the culminations of the civil rights movement: The Civil Rights Act of 1964, which prohibited discrimination on the basis of race, among other factors.[32]

The combination of these two developments made racial prejudice and discrimination against black people a taboo for most white people. To be racially prejudiced was to be associated with the images of the hateful, violent Southern white supremacists, who were viewed as immoral — and to be racially discriminatory was now illegal. Of course, most white people – like everyone else – want to see themselves as nice, moral individuals, and they recoil at any suggestion that they're otherwise. To claim or imply that a white person is racist or has done something racist can therefore cause them to feel unfairly insulted, judged or attacked, since they equate the concept with immorality.

Disguising Prejudices in Race-Neutral Language

In contemporary American society, it is no longer socially acceptable to openly express racial prejudices. As a result, most people have camouflaged these prejudices in race-neutral language, which has made prejudiced thinking difficult to detect and therefore rendered it largely unconscious.

---

[31] Bermanzohn, Sally Avery. "Violence, nonviolence, and the civil rights movement." *New Political Science* 22, no. 1 (2000): 31-48.
[32] Humphrey, Hubert H. *The Civil Rights Act of 1964: The passage of the law that ended racial segregation.* SUNY Press, 1997.

Consider the neighborhoods that Americans live in. Many of them are predominantly inhabited by one race or another — to the point where they can be called "white neighborhoods," "black neighborhoods," "Latino neighborhoods" and so on. Legally sanctioned segregation may be a thing of the past, but Americans are still highly segregated in where they choose to live — or rather, where white Americans choose to live.

Studies show that white people will flee a neighborhood if only 7 percent of its residents are black. The phenomenon is so well established that it even has a name: white flight.[33] However, if you asked most white people why they were doing it, they wouldn't openly say or even think to themselves that it's because of the presence of black people in their neighborhoods. They would say it was because those neighborhoods were becoming "dangerous" or "crime-ridden," which have become code words for describing black neighborhoods. On the other hand, they wouldn't say they wanted to live among other white people; they would say they wanted to live someplace "safe," "clean" or "sheltered," which have become code words for describing white neighborhoods.

This coded language makes it possible for white people to be racist without appearing racist. They can refrain from making a single mention of race, and yet they can still actively avoid living with black people and seek out living with fellow white people. As a result, many white people have few if any deep or ongoing relationships with black people, since they don't live in the same areas. The geography of where white people live makes them racially insulated.[34]

Society and culture then amplify this insulation further. From the schools they attend to the jobs they work, the movies and television shows they watch to the books they read, white people

---

[33] Kye, Samuel H. "The persistence of white flight in middle-class suburbia." *Social science research* 72 (2018): 38-52.

[34] DiAngelo, Robin J. "White fragility in racial dialogues." *Inclusion in urban educational environments: Addressing issues of diversity, equity, and social justice* 2, no. 1 (2006): 213.

are generally surrounded by white teachers, white employers, white celebrities and white authors, who dominate these platforms and positions of power, especially within predominantly white communities.

White Privilege

Being "privileged" doesn't necessarily mean "having it easy." Instead, it is simply an expression of the fact that, regardless of their circumstances, white people enjoy certain advantages because of their whiteness that people of color simply do not enjoy.

One of them is a sense of belonging. Everywhere a white person looks in his culture, he tends to see other white people: the leaders who filled his history textbooks, the authors of the novels he read in his English classes, the pictures of celebrities he sees in magazines, the directors and stars of the movies he watches and so forth. Of course, not all of these people are white — but they are predominantly white. By holding up these predominantly white figures as the exemplars of its culture, American society is depicting itself as a predominantly white society, thus sending an implicit message to white people: you belong here. On the flip side, it is sending the opposite message to colored people: you do not belong here.

Another advantage that white people have is a presumption of innocence until proven guilty. Because of racial prejudices that are reinforced by stereotypical depictions of black and Latino men in the media, white people tend to associate them with criminality. For instance, research shows that white people's perceptions of a neighborhood's crime level are directly correlated with how many young men of color live there.[35]

Research also shows that police and judges are susceptible to making this association as well, which leads to disproportionate

---

[35] Benjamin, Stacy E. "Color blind? The influence of race on perception of crime severity." *The Journal of Negro Education* 58, no. 3 (1989): 442-448.

arrests and prison sentences for black and Latino men compared to white men. Black men are unsympathetically branded as being inherently prone to crime, whereas Latino men are sympathetically excused as having had rough childhoods or as going through tough times. Thus, black and Latino men accused of crime are seen as hopeless cases who should be locked up to protect society, whereas white men are seen as redeemable and deserving of leniency.[36]

American Individualism, Meritocracy and Objectivity

There are a few other assumptions that play important roles in the formation of white fragility and lead people to deny the existence of racism and racial prejudice. Each of these assumptions builds on three of American society's predominant ideologies, which are the systems of ideas and ideals through which a society understands and justifies itself.

Two of these ideologies are closely related. The first is individualism, which holds that individuals can determine their own destinies without influence from the society around them, the circumstances into which they were born, or the groups to which they belong. The second is meritocracy, which holds that people get what they deserve, based on the merits of their skills and efforts.

In combination with each other, these ideologies allow people to justify the inequalities that exist between different racial groups. For instance, they allow white people to shrug their shoulders at statistics showing income disparities between white and black people. After all, according to meritocracy, if white people have more money than black people, they must have worked harder for it. And according to individualism, there's nothing stopping black people from working harder and catching up to white people, except their own gumption or lack thereof.

---

[36] Gruber, Aya. "Leniency as a miscarriage of race and gender justice." *Alb. L. Rev.* 76 (2012): 1571.

Thus, according to both of these ideologies, black people have no one but themselves to blame for their being economically unequal to white people.

The third ideology is objectivity, which holds that people can be free from biases in their understandings of the world. This ideology also dovetails with individualism, because the combination of the two allows white people to think it's possible for them to be free of racial biases.

On the one hand, individualism leads them to believe their view of the world is not influenced by the groups they belong to, one of which is a group called "white people." On the other hand, the ideology of objectivity leads them to believe they can be unbiased in their beliefs. Under the assumption that such an uninfluenced, unbiased state of mind is possible, white people can thus dismiss the notion that they might have racial biases by saying, "Oh, sure, other white people might have racial biases, but not me." In combination, these ideologies enable white Americans to deny racism on both a societal and a personal level.

Conclusion

White people in America are socialized into acquiring a set of racist assumptions and behavior patterns, which are wrapped up with some of the fundamental ideologies of American society. When their assumptions and patterns are challenged, they react in highly emotional ways, which prevent their racism from being addressed, thereby reinforcing it.

As a Caucasian, keep in mind the true nature of racism next time your beliefs, words or actions are questioned or cast as racist. Remember that it is not about you being a bad person or doing a bad thing; it is about you being born and raised in a systematically racist society, which has certain inescapable consequences, such as white privilege and racial biases. Try to use the occasion as an opportunity to examine, reassess and change your behavior and your way of seeing the world. It may make you feel uncomfortable, but that is part of the point; feeling comfortable about the topic of racism — or even worse, feeling entitled to feeling comfortable about it — is yet another aspect of white privilege for you to wrestle with, and getting out of your comfort zone is a precondition to grappling with any other aspects of it. Lastly, if you are a person of color, remember that it is not your responsibility to do this work for white people; they have to do it for themselves.

4
TRUE FEMINISM

Slavery and the Intensification of Sexism

In the nineteenth century, white American men — who used to see all women as sexual temptresses — came to see them as pure, innocent and virginal creatures. But this stereotype did not apply to black women, who they still assumed to be promiscuous. This attitude can be dated to the arrival of white colonizers from Europe. While establishing social and political order in America, they laid the foundations for racism and sexism. The colonizers labeled enslaved Africans as "sexual heathens." Black women were viewed as sexually immoral temptresses, while white women were perceived as pure. To white men, this baseless prejudice justified the rape of black women.[37]

While black men were subject to racism and exploitation, the added sexual exploitation of black women made their experiences far more demoralizing and dehumanizing. In addition to being forced to work in the fields alongside the men, women were also used as domestic house slaves, a means of breeding new slaves, and objects of sexual assault.

---

[37] Lerner, Gerda, ed. *Black women in white America: A documentary history*. Vintage, 1992.

Black Women's Systematic Devaluation

When slavery was finally abolished, black women found out that they had no opportunity to improve their own social standing or fight against their oppression. Their status as slaves may have changed, but the belief that black women were sexually promiscuous and immoral continued to pervade the American psyche.

A study of racist caricatures in the Atlantic magazine during the 1890s revealed that the "unchastity" of black women was attributed to their disregard of sexual purity, and the proof presented by the article's author for this disregard of sexual purity was the freedom with which white men could have their way with black women. It was not just journalists for the Atlantic who shared the view that black women invited sexual assault from white males. It was a view shared by white society as a whole and it affected how black women were treated.

It was not just the stereotype of sexual promiscuity that caused damage to black women. There was also the mythology of the black woman as a matriarch figure, spread and reinforced by white society. Due to their lower social status, black women worked tirelessly at low-paying service jobs to provide for their families. It was male social scientists who pointed out the role black women played in the labor and domestic spheres, labeling them matriarchs and heads of their households.

This matriarch label has been used by racist scholars to brainwash black women themselves. As a result, black women believe they have social and political power — economic security, reproductive rights and political clout. In reality, they possess none of these. In accepting their role as matriarchs, black women willingly accept their economic, sexist, and racist oppression, remaining submissive to the white patriarchal system.[38]

---

[38] Dobbins, Margaret Powell, and James Mulligan. "Black matriarchy: Transforming a myth of racism into a class model." *Journal of Comparative Family Studies* (1980): 195-217.

The Patriarchal Social Order

The American colonists have a lot to answer for. They introduced the idea of a patriarchal society, and the damage is still felt today. Patriarchy dictates that men assume the role of breadwinner and head-of-household — a concept which black men and women were subject to as much as their counterparts from other races and ethnicities.

This delineation of gender roles has been the cause of significant tension between black men and women. According to records dating as far back as 1852, prominent black figures such as black nationalist Martin Delaney advocated for distinct gender roles. He wrote that black men could enter business and women could be teachers but added that women should concern themselves foremost with rearing children.[39]

Racism from white employers stoked tensions further. From the early nineteenth century to the mid-twentieth century, whites refused to employ black men in wage-earning positions. This meant that black women needed to take on domestic service jobs to support their families. Under the white patriarchal structure, white men were the breadwinners. Because of this, black women also looked to black men to free them from their menial work – they would put pressure on their men to be upwardly mobile.

Such pressure also came from black writer Gail Stokes. In her 1968 essay on black relationships, Stokes expressed contempt for black men who did not embrace the breadwinner role.[40] She despised coming home to see her partner "looking like a slob." She then enviously reports to the maids, nannies and cooks that white husbands would provide for their wives.

It is no wonder black men felt powerless. In trying to reclaim their power, however, black men ended up degrading and controlling black women. As the racial hierarchy within patriarchy had long denied black men the right to status and power, most of

---

[39] Delaney, Martin. *The condition, elevation, emigration, and destiny of the Colored people of the United States.* Black Classic Press, 1993.
[40] Stokes, Gail. "Black woman to black man." *The Liberator,* December 17 (1968).

them were subjected to menial jobs with little monetary reward. Though black males were unable to find selfhood through work, they could assert their masculinity through violence against women.

And so black men adopted the traditionally white male sexual exploitation of black women. Malcolm X is a prime example. His biography depicts his exploitation of black women when he worked as a pimp. At the time, he justified this by claiming they were a threat to masculinity and needed to be dominated.[41]

The American Feminist Movement and its Inherent Racism

According to any dictionary definition, the word 'woman' describes all female humans. But the Women's Rights Movement's definition of 'woman' did not include all females. At the start of the movement, white women feared that black women — who they saw as immoral and promiscuous — would threaten their own social standing. It was an issue pointed out by the leader of the black New Era group, Josephine Ruffin. In her 1895 speech, Ruffin criticized white women's clubs refusal to admit black women due to "black female immorality."[42] This exclusion became the foundation of feminism, with the white feminist movement uniting to perpetuate this racist ideology.

In the early 1900s, the white women workers of the federal government advocated for segregation in workrooms, washrooms, and showers.[43] The Women's Rights Movement even used racist sentiment to bolster their own campaign for the right to vote.[44] A southern suffragist at the 1903 National American Woman's Suffrage Convention in New Orleans argued for the

---

41 Scharrer, Erica. "More than "just the facts"?: Portrayals of masculinity in police and detective programs over time." *Howard Journal of Communications* 23, no. 1 (2012): 88-109.

42 Ruffin, Josephine St Pierre. "Address to the first national conference of colored women." *The Woman's Era* 2, no. 5 (1895): 14.

43 Meier, August, and Elliott Rudwick. "The Rise of Segregation in the Federal Bureaucracy, 1900-1930." *Phylon (1960-)* 28, no. 2 (1967): 178-184.

44 Meringolo, Denise D. "African American Women in the Struggle for the Vote, 1850-1920." *American Studies International* 36, no. 3 (1998): 93.

enfranchisement of white women because it "would ensure immediate and durable white supremacy."

As a result of such racist rhetoric, the 1920s American suffrage movement was only committed to the interests of white middle and upper-class women.[45] Black women have been — and still are — erased from the feminist narrative, illustrating the unwillingness of white women to abandon their white supremacist foundations.

If any progress is to be made to bring down the white patriarchal social order, black and white women must unite. The women's liberation movement that emerged in the late 1960s struggled to gain the same privileges and power of white men. However, since white men are the ones holding power, in the end, it is they who choose who they share this power with. This means there is great competition between black and white women to be the "chosen" female group.

The white patriarchy has pitted the "moral" white woman against the "immoral" black woman to ensure both groups to remain subordinate to white men in the American power structure. American feminists must realize that their platform is inherently racist. In order to have a successful female revolution, white feminists must shatter this platform and strive to dispel any myths, stereotypes or dividing forces between women.

Black Women's Compromise

For as much as black liberation actually achieved, black women still did not enjoy the freedoms they had expected. American society was — and remains — oppressively imperialist, racist and sexist. Even on their way to achieving black liberation, black women took a back seat to black men. Male leaders of the Civil Rights Movement — Martin Luther King Jr, A. Philip Randolph and Roy Wilkins — overshadowed black women such

---

[45] Blee, Kathleen. "Women in White Supremacist Movements in the Century after Women's Suffrage." *100 Years of the Nineteenth Amendment: An Appraisal of Women's Political Activism* (2017).

as Rosa Parks, Daisy Bates and Fannie Lou Hamer.[46]

Though black male leaders no longer passively accepted the racist black matriarch myth, they did embrace the patriarchal gender roles established by white men and expected black women to be passive and subordinate. It was not just the leaders of the movement perpetuating the idea of the subservient woman. During the 1950s, black women were also socialized into adopting these gender roles through mass media, such as McCall's Magazine and Ladies Home Journal. These publications marketed make-up, clothes and feminine ideals to black women who were beginning to enter the middle classes. This indoctrination of black women through print media and television worked so well that decades later these constructed ideals of womanhood can still be seen. By the sixties and seventies, many black women believed black liberation had to be led by a strong black patriarchy. This belief was evident in the 1972 book Together Black Women, by Inez Smith Reid.[47]

In the book, black female interviewees share their views that black men should assume the dominant role in the black rights movement. As one respondent says, "I think the woman should be behind the man." The same woman thought that black men should lead black liberation because "men represent the symbol of the races."

Evidently, the core of each equality movement was rotten. The black liberation movement was inherently sexist and the concurrent feminist movement was racist.

Overturning the Promotion of American Masculine Ideals

Feminism is restricted within the white capitalist-patriarchal system. True feminism is the liberation of all people — men and women — from all domination, oppression and sexist role patterns. The only way to attain this is to completely restructure

---

46 Bair, Sarah. "The American Civil Rights Movement Reconsidered: Teaching the Role of Women." *The Social Studies* (2020): 1-9.
47 Reid, Inez Smith. *Together Black Women.* Emerson Hall Publishers, 1972.

American society.

The existing system promotes male brutality. The culture of violence against women will not be changed by creating more sanctuaries for victims of domestic abuse or teaching women to defend themselves against male sexual assault. Instead, society should stop promoting aggression and violence as masculine ideals. To advocate for the plight of all oppressed people, we must topple the individualist, imperialist, racist and sexist oppression that forms the bedrock of American society.

One way to go about this is to make sure the feminist movement stops operating within racist and classist confines. Members of women's rights organizations have not dared to address the exclusion that the feminist movement was founded on. Without acknowledging that some women experience sexist oppression to a far greater degree than others, radical change cannot happen.

The white capitalist patriarchal system is responsible for the whole ideology of sexist and racist oppression. White women and black men were encouraged to seek power for themselves within the rules of the existing patriarchy, rather than uniting across races and genders to achieve collective change and challenge white male dominance. This meant that black women struggled to find a voice in both the women's movement and the black liberation movement.

Conclusion

Black women have been oppressed for centuries, and this oppression even exists within the women's and black rights movements, which have further ostracized them. The only way to attain true equality is to topple all the existing power structures — of race, class and gender — so that any oppression or domination is eliminated. Black women, in particular, should lead this charge, as they have the most to gain as pioneers of this feminist movement.

5
UNCONSCIOUS BIASES

Implicit Association Test (IAT)

Unconscious bias essentially refers to the fact that people can unintentionally discriminate against others or have prejudicial beliefs they are not necessarily aware of.[48] However, since researchers found a way to measure unconscious bias it is now possible to increase this awareness.

Remarkably, studies have shown that the average person processes around 11 million pieces of information every second. Yet, we only process around 40 of those on a conscious level. You could therefore say that 99.999 percent of the information we take in gets processed unconsciously, and this would include our unconscious biases — the automatic associations we make based on accumulated information, such as associating black people with weapons and danger.

One way to measure unconscious bias is through an Implicit Association Test (IAT), an online test developed by Harvard psychologists Mahzarin Banaji, Anthony Greenwald and Brian

---

[48] Moule, Jean. "Understanding unconscious bias and unintentional racism." *Phi Delta Kappan* 90, no. 5 (2009): 320-326.

Nosek.[49] It measures the extent of your unconscious biases by asking you to react as quickly as possible to a series of questions that speak to your unconscious associations. For example, do you associate men or women with subjects like career and family or sciences and the arts? By requiring rapid decision-making, the test assesses your unconscious biases by tapping into your unconscious mind (not literally).

As you may suspect, many supposedly open-minded participants were shocked by their IAT results. Since the test went online in 2011, many people who identify as progressives and support gender equality have taken it. Yet, about 75 percent of all participants have shown a conservative-minded bias by strongly associating women with nurturing and household activities, and men with career and working. A similar bias was revealed regarding race, as 85 percent of white Americans associated black people with dangerous objects, such as knives and guns. Ultimately, people who were under the impression that they had no racial or gender bias had to face the surprising results of the test. This just proves how unconscious these biases truly are.

Discounting Privilege

How difficult do you think your childhood was? When considering your personal history, remember that white Americans, for example, generally have a much more privileged upbringing in terms of education, healthcare and standard of living than black Americans.

This might lead you to think that a reminder to keep things in perspective would result in more white Americans saying that their childhood was not so bad. However, when this question was posed in just this manner by Stanford psychologists in 2015, the opposite was true. White Americans actually emphasized the difficulty in their childhood more after being reminded of white

---

[49] Greenwald, Anthony G., Brian A. Nosek, and Mahzarin R. Banaji. "Understanding and using the implicit association test: I. An improved scoring algorithm." *Journal of personality and social psychology* 85, no. 2 (2003): 197.

privilege. In other words, people can accept that another group is disadvantaged while disregarding their own advantages. Most people end up maintaining the falsehood that they too had to overcome adversity. This is because people believe that acknowledging their privilege makes their achievements appear unearned or undeserved.

A similar trend exists in the workplace: another study revealed how employees with high salaries and benefits like quality healthcare and access to legal services were more likely to emphasize the strenuous effort and difficulty their job requires after they had been reminded about their perks of office. Interestingly enough, it has also been shown that people stop discounting their privileges when they are given a positive achievement to focus on. The 2015 Stanford study also revealed that the participants had different responses if, prior to being reminded of their privilege, they were asked to reflect on an impressive past accomplishment or given positive feedback on a test they had taken. Now, when asked about their childhoods, the participants were more likely to recognize their privilege, since they no longer felt that their sense of self-worth was under threat.

If you ever feel like someone needs a reminder about their privilege, you should remember to give them a compliment before confronting them. Otherwise, they will likely deny that privilege played a role in helping them get where they are today.

Identifying Unconscious Biases

What do unconscious biases look like? They are subtle, more pervasive than most people realize, and requires a lot of work to overcome them.

Take for instance the example of some black female executives — Funmi Williamson, Elizabeth Adefioye, Stacy Brown-Philpot, and Jo Ann Jenkins— who have had to feel excluded while in a room with other white female executives gathered in groups socializing. Those other groups were not necessarily rejecting them, rather playing into their unconscious biases and not recognizing them as fellow business executives since black businesswomen probably did not conform to their expectations. Similar incidents occur in the tech industry and also in academia where black female professors are more likely assumed to be of lower academic status.

Just because we have unconscious biases does not mean we have to accept them. With some effort, we can address them head-on and change how we interact with the world around us.

Countering Unconscious Biases

If you have ever overheard a racist comment and assumed it is not your place to speak up, you may want to think again. A 2003 study by psychologists Alexander Czopp and Margo Monteith showed that objections to racist statements were taken much more seriously when they came from other white people, rather than people of color.[50] According to the researchers this is because there is a common unconscious bias that associates privileged people with power and therefore when they counter a racist remark or behavior, it has a greater impact.

This is especially true in the workplace. In a 2016 study done by psychologists and management researchers, 350 North American executives were interviewed to assess how effective they were in promoting diversity within their teams.[51] After speaking with the executives, the researchers surveyed the executives' bosses to find out how they perceived the ongoing diversification efforts of their employees. The results showed that white male executives are routinely perceived in a positive light, whether or not they are successful in creating a diverse team. Meanwhile, executives who are women or people of color are far more likely to be harshly criticized. Not only that, but a white man

---

[50] Czopp, Alexander M., and Margo J. Monteith. "Confronting prejudice (literally): Reactions to confrontations of racial and gender bias." *Personality and Social Psychology Bulletin* 29, no. 4 (2003): 532-544.
[51] Hekman, David R., Stefanie K. Johnson, Maw-Der Foo, and Wei Yang. "Does diversity-valuing behavior result in diminished performance ratings for non-white and female leaders?" *Academy of Management Journal* 60, no. 2 (2017): 771-797.

can hire anyone he wishes — women, minorities or a team entirely made up of other white men — with little worry of receiving negative scrutiny from his boss. At the same time, a black person is likely to be criticized if they hire other black people, and a woman will be viewed negatively if she hires other women. Even if women and minority executives are promoting diversity in the company, they could still receive criticism for doing so.

Since white males have the power to enact change without getting in trouble, they have a greater responsibility to help curb racism and promote workplace diversity.

Developing Racial Identity Consciousness

American author Jodi Picoult sees herself as a progressive person, she was therefore taken aback when her son Kyle and his partner Kevin explained that she was sure to have unconscious racist biases based on her privileged white upbringing. Prior to this discussion, Picoult equated racism with the behavior of white supremacists. But Kyle and Kevin were eventually able to show Picoult how unconscious bias works. She became so eager to correct this lack of awareness that she enrolled in an anti-racism workshop. It was a lengthy process, but Picoult was able to start recognizing her own biases, and the experience led her to write her 2016 book *Small Great Things*[52] which is being adapted into a film starring Viola Davis and Julia Roberts.

Picoult's experience is quite typical, and it points to the three stages of changing your consciousness around racial identity. The first stage is denial. At this point, people must confront their misconceptions. But here is the problem: not only do many people refuse to believe they have any prejudices, they also think that racism in general no longer exists. This belief takes time to correct. The second stage is acceptance, and only some people will make it this far. By now, the person will have taken some active measures toward recognizing their biases. This is followed by the

---

[52] Picoult, Jodi. *Small great things: a novel.* Ballantine books, 2016.

third stage: deeper understanding. Here, white people can finally begin to understand that their experience is different from that of people of color. At this stage, a person will also question their own racial identity and what influence it has had on their life.

Conclusion

Unconscious biases are very real, even if the vast majority believe they have no prejudices. Research shows that many people have negative biases against people of color. We are also less willing to listen to advice that is not coming from a white man. It is possible, however, for all of us to increase our level of consciousness on matters of racial identity. To do so, we must be prepared to learn about what life is like for those who don't have our personal experience and be persistent in questioning our unconscious biases.

The media we take in is crucial to our perception of people, since it provides a window into worlds we are not familiar with. It is therefore beneficial to watch inclusive TV shows and movies. If we only engage with series that reflect a limited social reality, such as shows where all the characters belong to just one racial group and are heterosexual, our ability to understand other people decreases. Being picky about your media intake is an effective way to correct your unconscious biases.

6
GROWING PAINS

Economic Growth

Usually, countries desire economic growth because it brings more economic opportunities, upward mobility and increased living standards. A very good example of such growth is China. Over the last 40 years, China has grown economically to become the world's second-largest economy.[53] As of 2014, China's purchasing power parity – how much a country's money can buy in other countries – was $17.6 trillion, surpassing the United States' $17.4 trillion.

China's economic growth also brought economic opportunity. Its economy created new jobs, especially for the poor citizens in rural parts of the country; in just one generation, over 300 million Chinese were lifted out of poverty. In 2013, the Chinese State Council's income distribution plan made clear how the economy would be directed. China would work toward minimizing income inequality by raising low wages, increasing education spending and providing more affordable housing.[54]

---

[53] Liping, H. E. "China as the world's second largest economy: Qualifications and implications." *China and East Asia: After the Wall Street crisis* 33 (2013).
[54] Salidjanova, Nargiza. "China's new income inequality reform plan and implications for rebalancing." *US-China Economic and Security Review Commission, Washington, DC* (2013).

All of these therefore begs the question: what factors contribute to a country failing to grow? Take for instance the case of Argentina: when economic growth fails to materialize, it is often down to political instability and short-term thinking.

Back in 1913, Argentina was the world's tenth-richest country in terms of per capita income.[55] But between 1930 and the mid-1970s, there were six military coups in Argentina. While the political instability was happening, there were three separate bouts of hyperinflation that exceeded 500 percent per year and economic "growth" rates sank below zero for several years.[56]

In addition, successive administrations in Argentina during that period were not exactly thinking long-term about what could be done to benefit the country. They failed to invest in education and instead preferred to build up a cheap, poorly educated agricultural labor force – hardly a strategy for economic success. In fact, during the 1940s, Argentina had the lowest rate of secondary-school attendance in the world, and the result of poor education was ultimately a lack of innovation and a competitiveness shortfall.

The full effects were felt in Argentina's 1998–2002 economic and political crisis. Unemployment peaked at 25 percent, the currency lost 75 percent of its value and poverty went from 35 percent in 2001 to 54.3 percent in 2002.[57]

Threats to Economic Growth

If you are managing a household budget, going into debt can be terrifying. But when it comes to national economies, the situation is quite different – going into debt can actually stimulate economic growth.

---

[55] Salvatore, Ricardo D. "Stature decline and recovery in a food-rich export economy: Argentina 1900–1934." *Explorations in Economic History* 41, no. 3 (2004): 233-255.
[56] Peralta-Ramos, Monica. *The political economy of Argentina: power and class since 1930.* Routledge, 2019.
[57] Kehoe, Timothy J. "What can we learn from the 1998-2002 depression in Argentina?." *Great depressions of the twentieth century* (2007).

Take for instance the United States. After the World War II, the country took on a massive amount of debt to fund education, health care and infrastructure. A great deal of capital was put aside in 1956 for an expansive interstate highway system. The same was true of the 1944 G.I. Bill, which sought to educate and offer business loans to war veterans. As a result, over 2 million veterans attended college and over 5.5 million received training; this resulted in a significant improvement in the quality of the U.S. workforce.[58]

On the other hand, debt is not always a good thing. If it gets too high, trouble is around the corner – that much is clear from the 2007-2008 global financial crisis. As a result of high debt levels, Greece, Italy and Ireland all saw a decline in growth. Their interest payments on public debt increased to 10 percent of tax revenue, and any funds each government had needed to be redirected to debt repayment instead of developmental measures such as improving education. The debt crisis further hindered economic growth.[59]

There are other issues that restrict economic growth, however. For instance, global population growth increases the demand for natural resources, even as their finite supply dwindles. Within just 60 years, the world's population rose from 2.5 billion in 1950 to 7 billion in 2011 and it will probably reach 9 billion by 2050.[60]

As the world's resources are limited, commodity prices will inevitably rise and as these increases permeate through the economy, it is sure to result in inflation, which will in turn, negatively impact both the economy and individuals' living standards.

---

[58] Bennett, Michael J. *When Dreams Came True: The GI Bill and the Making of Modern America.* Brassey's, Inc., 1313 Dolley Madison Blvd., Suite 401, McLean, VA 22101, 1996.

[59] Iatridis, George, and Augustinos I. Dimitras. "Financial crisis and accounting quality: evidence from five European countries." *Advances in Accounting* 29, no. 1 (2013): 154-160.

[60] Leridon, Henri. "World population outlook: Explosion or implosion?." *Population Societies* 1 (2020): 1-4.

A good example is water. Even though 70 percent of the Earth is covered by water, about 97 percent of it is too salty to be used for drinking or irrigation. As demand for water rises with the population, water shortages are likely to thwart the cultivation of food and the generation of hydroelectricity in many countries. Global food markets and economic growth are therefore sure to suffer as a result of this shortage.

Automation and the Decline of the Global Workforce

It may seem counterintuitive, but one of the biggest threats an economy faces is people, and specifically its workforce – the people in an economy who actively contribute to its growth.[61]

In the developed world, both the quantity and quality of workforces are in decline, which poses a major problem. The core issue is aging populations, which the United Nations has identified as a global phenomenon. [62] According to the UN's forecasts, one in six people will be older than 65 by the year 2050, as compared to one in 12 in 2015.

An aging population raises the dependency ratio of retirees to workers, which in turn hampers productivity. With people living longer, we can expect longer retirements. This means more money will have to be spent on health care and pensions, which is no small economic burden.

In particular, developed nations are dealing with aging populations. Take Japan for instance: forecasts estimate that 40 percent of the country's population will be over the age of 65 by 2060. As Japan will have fewer younger workers, it will face labor shortages, decreased productivity and stagnating economic growth.

---

[61] Thompson, John A. "The contingent workforce: The solution to the paradoxes of the new economy." *Strategy & Leadership* 25, no. 6 (1997): 44-46.

[62] Rappaport, Anna, Ed Bancroft, and Lauren Okum. "The aging workforce raises new talent management issues for employers." *Journal of organizational excellence* 23, no. 1 (2003): 55-66.

Numbers are not the only problem, though: the quality of the workforce will decline too. Due to long-standing under-investment in education, the United States is already witnessing the start of this phenomenon. In the 2015 Program for International Student Assessment (PISA) test, 15-year-old American students ranked 13th out of 35 countries in math. When this generation of students joins the workforce, the United States will likely cease to remain competitive in technological innovation.

A further threat to the economy comes in the form of automation. Technology is increasingly rendering jobs redundant, which leads to greater income inequality.[63] A 2013 Oxford Martin School report estimated that 47 percent of all jobs in the United States were vulnerable to automation. The arrival of driverless vehicles was identified as particularly problematic. Interestingly, the trucking industry alone accounts for 3.4 to 4.5 million jobs in the United States. Therefore, truck, bus and taxi drivers could all be affected.

Critically, as technology will replace low-wage jobs first, this is sure to exacerbate income inequality. These same income disparities are also bound to increase the risk of social and political instability, as more people lose trust in the governmental and economic systems.

Protectionist Trade Policies

Two events in 2016 seemed to indicate that the global economic consensus was turning a corner. First, the United Kingdom voted to leave the European Union in the Brexit referendum. Then, later in the year, Donald Trump was elected President of the United States. These indicate that the world is steering away from globalization and back to protectionism. The Brexit scenario was a referendum on a UK-first protectionist policy while the outcome of the U.S. election was a similar

---

[63] Hornborg, Alf. *The power of the machine: Global inequalities of economy, technology, and environment.* Vol. 1. Rowman Altamira, 2001.

referendum on President Trump's America-first campaign promises.

Unfortunately, protectionist trade policies damage both global and national economies alike. The global economy struggles because protectionist tariffs and quotas on imported goods and services end up limiting trade and thus squeezing the flow of cross-border capital.[64]

Ironically, national economies are the second victim of protectionism. Take for instance the 1930 Smoot-Hawley Tariff Act, which enforced an effective tax rate of 60 percent on over 3,200 products imported into the United States.[65] Theoretically, protectionist policies are meant to safeguard local businesses and therefore bolster the domestic economy, but the Smoot-Hawley Tariff Act did not achieve this goal at all. Instead, other countries retaliated by imposing tariffs on American products. The result was job losses and lower living standards: America's GDP plummeted from $104.6 billion in 1929 to only $57.2 billion in 1933.

On top of that, protectionism negatively affects producers in developing countries, with EU and U.S. farm subsidies constituting prime examples. Although these measures were designed to subsidize domestic farmers in the domestic market, farmers in South America, Africa and Asia naturally struggle to compete in those markets. Consequently, agricultural trade in developing countries is unable to bring in money that could be used for building infrastructure and the like. In addition, developing countries account for more than 80 percent of the world's population.

A third consequence of protectionism is global labor imbalance. According to the International Labour Organization, globally there are 73.4 million people between the ages of 18 and

---

[64] Irwin, Douglas A. "The false promise of protectionism: Why Trump's trade policy could backfire." *Foreign Aff.* 96 (2017): 45.

[65] Eichengreen, Barry. *The political economy of the Smoot-Hawley tariff.* No. w2001. National Bureau of Economic Research, 1986.

24 who are unemployed. Simultaneously, however, there are also labor shortages in developed countries, such as Japan, due to their aging populations.

One way to deal with labor shortages is to enforce effective immigration policies. Canada and Australia faced just this problem and they tackled it by bringing in labor from countries that had a surplus. They accomplished this by establishing a points-based system, which was designed to judge migrants on their academic achievements and work experience.

The Risks of State Intervention

Hundreds of millions of people in the developing world live on less than a dollar a day. When the biggest concern is whether there will be food on the table every night, it is understandable that calls for political freedom become secondary. That is why many people in the world prioritize economic growth over a flawless, transparent democracy.[66]

China is also an excellent example in this regard. It has developed a form of authoritarian state capitalism that has served the country well by fostering economic growth. It does this by prioritizing collectivism over individual rights and freedoms. Record economic growth there has resulted in a reduction in poverty that is historically unprecedented. [67]

One key strategy of the Chinese government in reducing income inequality is to increase spending on affordable housing and education. Chinese secondary school attendance currently stands at 94 percent, which is mind-boggling considering that it was just 28 percent in 1970.

The government has also established an impressive infrastructure initiative. As a result of an ever-expanding network

---

[66] Xi, Jinrui, and Christopher Primiano. "China's Influence in Asia: How Do Individual Perceptions Matter?." *East Asia (Piscataway, Nj)* (2020): 1.
[67] Ibid.

of highways built in the last 15 years, China now has more paved roads than the United States.

Not all that glitters is gold, however. As amazing as China's success appears at first glance, excessive government control and intervention can actually endanger long-term economic growth in reality. The George W. Bush administration ran into just that problem. Through its "Housing for All" policy, the U.S. government tried to incentivize American households to invest their wealth in housing instead of stocks, goods and cash. To do so, the government essentially started participating in financial markets, acting as a de facto mortgage lender. It offered affordable mortgages through two government-sponsored enterprises known as Fannie Mae and Freddie Mac. Many Americans ended up buying property they could not afford and found themselves burdened by crippling debt; these very transactions played a key role in triggering the cataclysmic 2008 financial crisis.[68]

It just goes to show that emerging economies should be aware of the weaknesses of an economic system built on state intervention. State-centric system such as China's will not be able to print money forever.

Forcing the Issue

The last decade has seen the rise of populism and growing economic uncertainty; it has become increasingly clear that Western democracies have to adapt. Radical reforms are needed to ensure that good decision-making remains a key pillar in Western democracies and it is the responsibility of the citizens to actually force the issue.

First of all, we need to make it difficult for policymakers to easily revoke legislation. As things stand, it is fairly straightforward for policymakers to void their predecessors' decisions. This changeability of policy creates uncertainty that discourages

---

[68] Acharya, Viral V., Matthew Richardson, Stijn Van Nieuwerburgh, and Lawrence J. White. *Guaranteed to fail: Fannie Mae, Freddie Mac, and the debacle of mortgage finance.* Princeton University Press, 2011.

investment, which, in turn, is detrimental to long-term economic growth. Take for example the Paris Agreement on climate change. President Barack Obama signed it in December 2015 to great fanfare, only for his successor, Donald Trump, to withdraw in 2017.

It is clear, then, that what is needed are international agreements that bind governments to already signed policies. This might include agreements made by the World Trade Organization (WTO) or NATO security agreements.

Secondly, we should ensure that campaign contributions are strictly limited. That way, the disproportional impact of wealthy interest groups on democratic elections can be constrained. An estimated – and mind-boggling – $2 billion was raised in campaign contributions during the 2016 U.S. presidential election cycle. Campaign contributions in the United States have skyrocketed in successive elections, and this has resulted in a political system in which wealth is the only thing that matters. Politicians have adjusted their policies to benefit rich donors instead of the voting public at large.

Third, policymakers should be paid more. That way, working in the public sector will be more attractive to talented people. As things stand, the significant pay gap between private and public sectors means that the public sector is left looking like the poorer- and less skilled-cousin. By way of comparison, the average CEO's income in the United States increased tenfold from $1.5 million to $15 million between 1979 and 2013. As for the President of the United States' wage package? It rose marginally from $100,000 in 1969 to $400,000 in 2001.

Reforming the Political System

Reforming the political system is no easy task, but it is a necessary one and there are three more aspects that need changing.

First, politicians' terms in office should be extended, but with strictly enforced term limits. Longer terms in office will allow leaders to focus on long-term solutions due to increased accountability. For this, Mexico is a good example. Francisco Madero won the country's presidential election in 1910, campaigning under the slogan, "Valid voting and no reelection." Since then, Mexican presidents have only been able to hold a single six-year term in office, once. The result has been a relatively stable political environment and high rates of economic growth compared to Mexico's Latin American neighbors.

Secondly, there needs to be some sort of minimum requirement for candidates, particularly in terms of "real-world" experience. Take for example the British House of Commons. A 2012 study by the British House of Commons Library showed that the percentage of parliamentary representatives with backgrounds in manual labor dropped dramatically from over 70 percent to 25 percent between 1983 and 2010. We should recognize that politicians who lack such "real-world" experience tend to lack understanding and empathy for people facing real economic challenges. They are more likely to make policy decisions in favor of the upper classes – or basically whatever it takes to keep their seats in parliament. Therefore, we should stipulate that in order to run for office, a candidate should already serve a certain number of years of work outside the political sphere.

Finally, voting needs to be mandatory. According to the International Institute for Democracy and Electoral Assistance, only 36 percent of eligible voters in the United States voted during the midterm elections in November 2014. It was the lowest turnout in over 70 years and became part of a startling trend.

Since voters are fundamentally responsible for electing politicians and the policies they implement, it is essential that turnout is increased. Fines are one way this might be achieved, and Australia has such a system. Over there, you are fined $20 the first time you don't vote, and $50 for each subsequent no-show on election days. That has made the country's turnout rate during elections to be more than 90 percent. Singapore and Belgium also enforce compulsory voting.

All these countries are on their way to ensuring that their democracies survive way into the future.

Conclusion

We need long-term economic growth to achieve higher living standards, which encompass everything from increased wages and better education, to reduced income inequality and access to health care. However, current liberal democracies are beginning to favor short-term policies and protectionism. If we do not manage to steer our democracies away from this path, economic stagnation and lower standards of living are sure to follow.

7
IMPLICIT GENDER BIASES

Default Genders & Emoji Equality

For a long time, women have been overlooked because humans have been conditioned to see the male gender as the default gender.[69] In 1889, archaeologists uncovered an armored Viking skeleton in Sweden. Despite the skeleton's female pelvic bone, they assumed that the bones belonged to a male warrior, and for over 125 years, no one noticed this misidentification error until DNA evidence provided crucial evidence in 2017.[70]

In *On the Generation of Animals* (340 BC), Aristotle described men as normal and women as aberrations.[71] In anatomy, the male body was historically the default; if the female body was considered at all, it was the exception. Some female organs, such as the ovaries, were not even named until the seventeenth century.

---

[69] Corbett, Greville G., Norman M. Fraser, and B. Unterbeck. "Default genders." *Gender in Grammar and Cognition: I. Approaches to Gender, II. Manifestations of Gender* (1999): 55-97.

[70] Hedenstierna-Jonson, Charlotte, Anna Kjellström, Torun Zachrisson, Maja Krzewińska, Veronica Sobrado, Neil Price, Torsten Günther, Mattias Jakobsson, Anders Götherström, and Jan Storå. "A female Viking warrior confirmed by genomics." *American Journal of Physical Anthropology* 164, no. 4 (2017): 853-860.

[71] Lawrence, Cera R. "On the Generation of Animals, by Aristotle." *Embryo Project Encyclopedia* (2012).

Interestingly, gender bias is not an ancient concept. Something as contemporary as emojis still privileges masculinity. All emojis are assigned by a single company — Unicode, but it is up to each emoji-supporting platform to determine how they depict Unicode's emojis. Before 2016, Unicode did not assign genders to emoji symbols; they simply stipulated that emoji symbols should include, for example, a runner or a police officer. The platforms chose to depict male runners and male police officers. It was only when Unicode began to assign gendered emoji symbols that women and men achieved "emoji equality."[72]

Gender Datasets

Women's needs are usually overlooked at the policy level because several policies — whether corporate or governmental — are set by men. Facebook's Chief Operating Officer Sheryl Sandberg was not the first Facebook employee to get pregnant, but she was the first pregnant executive. She then realized that the company needed priority parking for pregnant women. Until Sandberg's pregnancy, the executive suite simply hadn't considered the needs of pregnant employees.

Leaving women out of the dataset creates a gender data gap that privileges men. Take for instance, European public transport. Men are more likely to hold full-time jobs than women, and transport data therefore focuses on mobility related to full-time employment, as a 2012 EU-wide study found. The result was a transport system that directs resources to peak travel times, without prioritizing non-commuter travel. The gender data gap leaves female transport users underserved, and even penalizes them for the way they travel. Women use public transport differently from men, but transport data fails to take this into account. Ticket prices are often set by journey, not distance: men are likely to make a two-trip standard commute. Part-time workers

---

[72] Klafke, Raquel Forma, and Daniela Kutschat Hanns. "The Digital Evolution of Gender." In *International Conference on Human-Computer Interaction*, pp. 409-414. Springer, Cham, 2018.

and caregivers — again, mostly women — usually "trip-chain," making a number of short trips throughout the day. The result is that women end up paying more to travel shorter distances.

Planning, Design and the Female Experience

If you have ever attended a concert, church service, state fair or other public event and compared the line for the ladies' bathrooms with that for the men, you will probably have noticed a disparity between the two. Those long lines are a direct result of the gender data gap: public planning regulations frequently stipulate that venues allocate equal bathroom space for men and women. This looks good on paper — but a closer look reveals that this planning decision is based on data that ignores women's needs. Women and men use bathrooms differently, but bathroom design fails to account for this. With a mix of urinals and cubicles, male bathrooms can offer more facilities than female bathrooms in the same allocated space, even though women do more in the bathroom: women are more likely to accompany children to the bathroom; women usually require more time to clean the toilet seat, or cover it with tissue paper; menstruating women might need to change their tampons or sanitary pads; and pregnant women urinate more frequently. Those long lines are the result of design flaws arising from incomplete data.

What is merely an inconvenience in the developed world can have far more serious consequences in the developing world. In homes without a private bathroom, access to facilities is an issue for both genders, but a lack of public bathrooms poses more problems for women. Where a bathroom is unavailable, men relieve themselves in public, but it is physically difficult and often socially taboo for women to do the same. Some women hold in their urine, which can lead to health issues, such as urinary tract infections and dehydration.

Without access to a private toilet, women in the developing world rely on public bathrooms, which are rarely female-friendly. They are often in unsafe locations and not segregated by gender.

This means that when women leave their houses to use public bathrooms, they run the risk of sexual assault and violence. In India, women without access to a private toilet are twice as likely to experience non-partner sexual violence compared to women with bathrooms in their homes. These women are disadvantaged by bathroom designs that neglect their physical needs and safety.

Women's Health and Safety

When it comes to health and safety, the word "standard" more often means "standard male"; as a result, many health and safety guidelines leave women out in the cold. This is certainly the case when it comes to the recommended office temperature, which was set in the 1960s, based on the metabolic resting rate of a 40-year-old, 155-pound male — leaving women working in offices up to five degrees too cold for the average female metabolic rate.

Cars undergo stringent safety testing before they are put on the market. But the crash test dummies required for those tests are all male. Dummies have been used since the 1950s, and, even today, the typical dummy's dimensions remain in the 50th percentile for males. It is 5ft 10in tall and weighs 168 pounds, has a male spine and male muscle proportions.

Due to their anatomy and size, women tend to sit differently and wear seatbelts differently from men. In crash tests carried out with male dummies, it is therefore impossible to gather accurate data on women's specific safety outcomes. Some car companies do use anatomically correct female dummies — but they are not legally required to do so. In the EU, none of the five safety tests a car must pass before being allowed on the market stipulates that a female crash test dummy should be used — even though, according to a 2011 study, women are 47 percent more likely than men to be seriously injured when they are involved in car crashes.

The auto industry assumes that the male body is standard. So does science. Just as the auto industry carries out tests on male dummies, many scientific studies test their findings on reference man.[73] Who is reference man? According to the International Commission on Radiological Protection's 1974 definition:

"Reference man is defined as being between 20–30 years of age, weighing 155 pounds, is 5ft 6in in height, and lives in a climate with an average temperature between 50°F to 68°F. He is a Caucasian and is a Western European or North American in habitat and custom."

Historically, scientific studies have used reference man to represent everyone. This is especially problematic when it comes to health and safety in the workplace. Not only are women's bodies proportionally and anatomically different from male bodies, they have different immune systems and hormones. These differences affect how women's bodies tolerate exposure to radiation and industrial chemicals. And yet many health and safety recommendations are based on reference man. As a result, female workers are being exposed to chemicals at levels that may not be harmful to men but are certainly harmful to women. A 2014 study shows that women are more affected by radiation exposure than men. And women exposed to EDCs (endocrine-disrupting chemicals) in the workplace have a 42 percent increased risk of breast cancer.

GDP and Gender Gap

The biggest gender gap of all occurs on a global scale — in the way we measure gross domestic product (GDP). The GDP measures national output in terms of goods and services. Domestic work, childcare, and eldercare are services typically performed by women. When this domestic and care work is unpaid, it is not factored into GDP. Yet it has economic value — when a woman performs this unpaid work, she is usually supporting a partner whose income is counted toward GDP.

---

[73] Snyder, W. S., L. R. Karhausen, G. Parry Howells, and I. H. Tipton. *Report of the task group on reference man.* Vol. 23. Oxford: Pergamon, 1975.

According to the World Bank, Great Britain had a GDP of £2.7 trillion in 2016. Numbers from the UK's Office for National Statistics show that, when unpaid work is included, that number goes up to about £3.9 trillion. The United Nations estimates that in the U.S. in 2012, $3.2 trillion worth of unpaid childcare was performed. The value of that unpaid care work was equal to 20 percent of the country's $16.2 trillion GDP for that year. Similarly, an Australian study from 2017 found that if unpaid childcare were counted toward GDP, it would actually constitute Australia's largest industry.

When this work is not factored into the GDP, it is not properly quantified. And without properly quantifying women's unpaid work, it is difficult to support women in performing paid work.

At the moment, unpaid work is creating a gender employment gap that slows the economy. When women participate in the labor force, economies grow. Between 1970 and 2009, the female labor force increased by roughly 38 million. This increase, says the McKinsey Global Institute, generated approximately 25 percent more GDP. McKinsey also suggests that, were women to participate in the labor force at a rate equal to men, global GDP would swell to $12 trillion.

A significant factor preventing us from closing the current 27 percent gender gap in employment is unpaid domestic and care work. In Europe, where there is currently a 12 percent gender employment gap, 25 percent of surveyed women stated that care work prevents them from joining the labor force. Only three percent of men said the same.

Gathering data on women's unpaid work would allow governments to make policy decisions that support women entering the labor force, benefiting both women and the economy. This could take the form of increased spending on social infrastructure like affordable childcare and eldercare — spending that would actually generate jobs and increase GDP. In the U.S., a two percent GDP investment in social infrastructure would create 13 million more jobs, compared to 7.5 million jobs if the same amount were invested in construction.

Political Systems and Public Policies

The gender data gap comes about when we assume that one gender, in this case the male gender, is the default, and that these needs are standard needs. This has proven so persistent because many people making high-level data-based decisions are male. In politics, men far outnumber women, which is a serious problem: statistics show that female politicians are far more likely to address the gender gap in their policies than their male counterparts.

Women are significantly underrepresented in politics.[74] In December 2017, only 23.5 percent of the world's politicians were women. One reason that more women are not entering politics is probably because the current underrepresentation leads to the perception of politics as a "male" space, which is bad news for women. In 2008, researchers at the University of California, Berkeley concluded that when a woman speaks in a stereotypically male context — such as Wall Street, for example — she is judged more negatively than a man who says exactly the same thing. Women in the political sphere are deemed aggressive whereas men are deemed assertive. This influences their likeability, which in turn affects their electability.

Given their negative public perception, it is unsurprising that female politicians are more frequently the targets of gendered abuse than male politicians. A global IPU report found that, in 2016, 66 percent of female politicians reported misogynistic abuse from male peers. Female politicians are also subjected to online abuse. In Australia, an astounding 80 percent of women over 30 reported they would not run for office due to online harassment of female politicians.

---

[74] Paxton, Pamela Marie, Melanie M. Hughes, and Tiffany Barnes. *Women, politics, and power: A global perspective.* Rowman & Littlefield Publishers, 2020.

This hostility can make entering politics, not to mention staying there, a difficult proposition for women. Unfortunately, we cannot rely on male politicians to legislate for gender equality. Female politicians are far more likely than their male peers to address the gender gap. A 2016 study of British female politicians showed that they brought women's issues to the table more consistently than their male counterparts. Female MPs talked more about family policy, education, and social infrastructure.

In addition, women politicians translate their talk into action. An analysis of female politicians in Organization for Economic Cooperation and Development (OECD) countries between 1960 and 2005 found that they were more likely to create and support policies focused on women. A 2004 study in India backs this up: When a third of local council seats were reserved for female candidates, investment in infrastructure connected to women's needs increased.

When women do come to political power, they are active in enacting policies that recognize and accommodate women's needs. Ironically, politics itself has a gender data gap; until we reach gender parity among our political representatives, it is statistically unlikely that women's issues will be given the weight they deserve.

Conclusion

Thanks to the gender data gap, we live in a world with a serious design flaw: it is made for men. As long as we continue to assume the male gender and male needs are "standard," we will continue to create a world that disenfranchises women. Addressing the gender data gap is an important step on the road to achieving gender equality. It is important to be mindful of the gender data gap and to ensure that we are not perpetuating it.

8
A HISTORY OF RACIAL CRIMINALIZATION

Vote "No" on Marijuana Reform…

In 1975, Washington DC, had a black mayor, a majority-black city council, and a resident population that was about 70% black. That same year, the city made a decision that would stigmatize young black males for decades to follow — proposals were made to soften marijuana-related legislation due to concerns about racial injustice.[75]

In the early 1970s, 80% of DC residents arrested for marijuana possession were black, and those arrests held a lifelong burden since they had to be reported on housing, schooling and employment applications.[76] Therefore, on March 18, 1975, David Clarke, a member of the city council, proposed the Marijuana Reform Act, which sought to lower the penalties for possession of marijuana to a fine and a citation. The black community headed by fellow council member Doug Moore, however, opposed the

---

[75] Roffman, Roger A. "Marijuana and its control in the late 1970's." *Contemp. Drug Probs.* 6 (1977): 533.
[76] Nunn, Kenneth B. "Race, crime and the pool of surplus criminality: or why the war on drugs was a war on blacks." *J. Gender Race & Just.* 6 (2002): 381.

proposal, arguing that easing penalties would make it easier for black people to succumb to crime and addiction. The opposition was successful, and on October 21, 1975, the Reform Act was tabled.

To help understand the seemingly irrational reasoning behind this opposition to the marijuana reform, it is important to examine the heroin epidemic in the 1960s.

In the early to mid-1960s, less than 3 percent of new prisoners at the Central Detention Facility in Washington DC were heroin addicts. Then came a huge spike in usage, and by June 1969, this figure had grown to 45 percent, with the majority of addicts being young black men. There was a strong link between heroin addiction and crime — addicts typically resorted to criminal means to be able to afford their drugs. According to one study, heroin addicts in DC and three other U.S. cities committed an annual average of more than 300 crimes.[77]

The spike in criminal activity led to outrage across black communities, and black drug dealers were deemed to be betraying their race. Some even believed that black heroin addicts and their passive dependence benefited the white community. In May 1969, posters that likened heroin addiction to slavery appeared across DC, printed by the anti-drug organization Blackman's Development Center.[78]

Gun Laws

While the DC city council was discussing penalties for marijuana possession in 1975, gun violence was rising. In 1974, it was the number one cause of death for males in Washington under the age of 40, and this spike led to the city council discussing tougher gun-control measures.[79]

---

[77] DuPont, Robert L., and Mark H. Greene. "The dynamics of a heroin addiction epidemic." *Science* 181, no. 4101 (1973): 716-722.
[78] DuPont, Robert L. "Heroin addiction treatment and crime reduction." *American Journal of Psychiatry* 128, no. 7 (1972): 856-860.
[79] Ludwig, Jens, and Philip J. Cook, eds. *Evaluating gun policy: Effects on crime and violence.* Brookings Institution Press, 2004.

Councilman John Wilson suggested that the sale, purchase and possession of all shotguns and handguns be banned and that the maximum sentencing guidelines for people convicted of gun crimes be raised. Furthermore, he proposed that minimum sentencing times be introduced so that more offenders would go to jail. Wilson's proposals were supported by victims of gun-related crime and residents who were angered by the fact that, at the time, 85 percent of those killed by guns were black.

Fellow councilman Doug Moore, however, opposed Wilson's suggestions, claiming that guns were crucial for the black community to arm themselves against street criminals and racism-fueled violence. In 1976, the council passed stricter gun-control laws, with everyone in favor except Moore. Though the new laws were not as strict as those Wilson had proposed, they nonetheless banned further sales of guns and mandated the registration of existing ones. Many black citizens were in favor of the new laws, in part due to the perception that black-on-black street crime had become a greater threat to the community than racist violence.[80]

It can be argued that the stricter gun laws were a huge victory for civil rights; black policymakers passed legislation that aimed to protect the lives of black citizens. Unfortunately, however, the policy change was not as effective as many people had hoped. The new laws and penalties mostly punished poorly educated black men from low-income households, while still failing to protect the larger black community against gun violence. This was likely because of the overemphasis on punishment, rather than addressing the root causes of gun crimes, such as racial inequality in the provision of health care, education and employment.

Hiring More Black Officers

Throughout most of U.S. history, racism has prevented black people from being considered for positions of authority, especially

---

[80] Ackah, Yaw. "Fear of crime among an immigrant population in the Washington, DC metropolitan area." *Journal of Black Studies* 30, no. 4 (2000): 553-573.

in police departments. This meant that significant efforts were required to increase the number of black people on the police force. In the late 1940s, black civilians started to join the police force. However, segregation existed in patrol cars, and black officers did not have equal career tracks. To apply for a promotion, you needed to have good written test scores and be assigned a high "suitability for promotion" rating by your supervisors. Unfortunately, racism prevented black officers from receiving good suitability ratings, which made it near impossible to get a promotion.

Two black officers, Burtell Jefferson and Tilmon O'Bryant, could not get promoted due to their low suitability ratings. Therefore in 1958, they formed a covert class for black officers, since very high test scores were the only way to compensate for low suitability ratings. After six months, 12 out of the 15 officers in the class scored high enough on the test to receive a promotion.

Although this was an important step forward for black policing, having more black officers did not really reduce police violence. Furthermore, black officers were not necessarily more sympathetic toward black citizens. A 1966 study by the University of Michigan looked at both white and black officers on duty, and though black officers were not as prejudiced as white ones, 28 percent of them were still classified as "prejudiced" or "highly prejudiced."

One reason for the high percentage was class divisions. Officers tended to perceive poor black people as posing a risk to law and order in black communities. In some instances, that concern turned into over-zealousness, which resulted in the use of excessive force for minor offenses such as loitering and drunkenness.

Drug Crime Sentences

Starting in the late 1930s, all drug crimes in DC received a minimum one-year sentence, and a repeat offense fetched ten years behind bars. By the 1970s however, drug dealing became so rampant in the city, that the city council passed new drug-related legislation in March 1981.

David Clarke, the chairman of the council's Judiciary Committee, proposed the categorization of drugs into groups with specific penalties. For instance, marijuana dealers would receive a maximum one-year sentence, while cocaine and heroin dealers would get sentences of up to five and ten years, respectively. Clarke's suggestion was a response to contemporary public perception, which viewed the legal system as a revolving door that returned criminals to the streets.

African-American councilmember John Ray opposed Clarke's proposal with a stricter one, which sought to raise the maximum sentences even more, to three, ten and 15 years for marijuana, cocaine and heroin dealing respectively. Ray also proposed mandatory minimum sentences for gun and drug offenses. The decision regarding maximum sentencing fell in Ray's favor; however, the council rejected his minimum sentencing proposal.

Regardless, a ballot in January 1982 established mandatory minimum sentences for drug dealing. Initiative 9 mandated that anyone convicted of dealing heroin would get a minimum of four years in prison, while selling cocaine or marijuana would result in two years and one year in prison respectively.

This initiative was strongly supported by Ray, along with police chief Burtell Jefferson, but opposed by a wide range of groups concerned with civil liberties. So Ray and Jefferson cleverly capitalized on the rage of DC residents over the booming drug market. Some weeks prior to the vote for Initiative 9, Ray and Jefferson campaigned by visiting one murder scene after another, demonstrating to the public that crime was a huge problem in DC. On September 14, 1982, Initiative 9 won by a landslide.

Though the policy had no impact on crime reduction, drug-related prosecutions increased by nearly 300 percent between 1982 and 1984.

Warrior Policing

By the late 1980s, the war on drugs was well and truly underway, and police were trained as though they were soldiers going into battle. Thus, they began to instinctively see young people from neighborhoods with high incidences of crime as potential enemies who could attack at a moment's notice.

Warrior policing came about as a result of the crack cocaine epidemic.[81] Crack cocaine is made by heating cocaine, baking soda and water, and it creates an immediate and intense high that can be highly addictive. In 1984, 15% of people taken in by DC cops tested positive for cocaine. Three years later, that percentage had grown to 60%, with nearly all of them having smoked crack.[82]

The black community also experienced the destructiveness of crack, with a representative from the National Association for the Advancement of Colored People (NAACP) claiming it was "the worst thing to hit us since slavery."

Due to a growing fear of the drug, many members of the black community were in favor of heavy-handed policing. Drug-related violence was up, and drug cartels and heavily armed street thugs were increasing in numbers. Predictably, the violence was far from evenly distributed — in 1989, 90% of homicide victims in Washington DC, were black.

Stop and Search

By 1995, incidences of violence in DC had started to drop after peaking during the crack epidemic. However, homicide rates were still three times higher than in 1985. On January 13th of that year, Eric Holder, an African-American U.S. attorney for Washington DC, pointed out that 94% of black victims were murdered by another black person.

As a solution to rising homicide rates, Holder came up with

---

[81] Adachi, Jeff. "Police Militarization and the War on Citizens." *Hum. Rts.* 42 (2016): 14.
[82] Miller, Richard Lawrence. *Drug warriors and their prey: From police power to police state.* Greenwood Publishing Group, 1996.

Operation Ceasefire, which made "stop and search" an official police policy.[83] The program leveraged the city's numerous traffic regulations, which meant that the police had an excuse to stop almost any vehicle. This allowed them to search cars for illegal weapons to be confiscated. Most studies however show that only 1–5% of the searches resulted in weapons being seized, meaning that a large proportion of innocent citizens were stopped for no justifiable reason.[84]

Another problem with Operation Ceasefire was that it disproportionately affected black neighborhoods. For example, the program did not apply to the city's Second District, one of DC's more prosperous, white neighborhoods, due to its low rate of gun violence. And because police officers would frequent black neighborhoods, black drivers were significantly more likely to be stopped by the police. These stops often resulted in arrests for crimes not even linked to guns, such as drug possession. This, despite the fact that black drivers were not more likely to possess drugs than white drivers.

This variance did not surprise Holder. He knew from the very beginning that young black men would be stopped more frequently, especially those in poor areas. Between 1996 and 1997, sociologist Ronald Weitzer found that people living in lower-class black areas were four to seven times more likely to report pretextual stops and police abuse than those living in middle-class black areas. The "stop and search" tactic was just another component of the war on drugs that only increased the imprisonment of black people.

Conclusion

Legislation enacted as part of the war on drugs in Washington DC, such as warrior policing and "stop and search" tactics,

---

[83] Rubin, Joel. "Stopping crime before it starts." *Los Angeles Times* 21 (2010).
[84] Bowling, Ben, and Coretta Phillips. "Disproportionate and discriminatory: Reviewing the evidence on police stop and search." *The Modern Law Review* 70, no. 6 (2007): 936-961.

resulted in higher rates of police violence and incarceration rates that disproportionately affected black people. Even more surprising: the black community itself appealed for stricter penalties for many crimes. However, policy changes and new laws since the mid-1970s have not only failed to reduce crime rates; they have also helped to marginalize black people further.

9

THREATS TO DEMOCRACY

Democracy & American Politics

Democracy is a system of government for the people, by the people. In 1789, the U.S. Constitution brought together democratic ideals of equality and fair representation in a radical way. Unfortunately, the values embedded in the Constitution were ignored for much of the country's early history, and the United States had a weak and deeply corrupt political system right up until the 19th century. Goods and services were bought and sold in exchange for political alliances and, unsurprisingly, it was the rich and influential who wielded the most political power.

Towards the end of the 19th century, however, things began to change. The U.S. federal government began to experience a series of transformations, and by mid-20th century, it had become an independent, effective and value-driven political actor. This transformation began with the Progressive Movement, led by politicians such as Theodore Roosevelt, who broke up big business conglomerates. This work was pushed along by the politics of the New Deal, which provided U.S. citizens with healthcare and a general pension.[85]

Industrialization had also altered traditional social structures and was a driving force behind social changes. From African-Americans to suffragettes, a host of newly empowered political actors began to shake up the old and corrupt system. By 1989, it looked like democracy was on top — the fall of Communism in Eastern Europe appeared to solidify democracy's triumph, and its consistent global expansion seemed to be the inevitable path that the future would take.[86]

In fact, between 1970 and 2010, the number of democracies across the globe increased from 35 to nearly 120, about 60 percent of the world's countries. But as democracy spread, it encountered its fair share of challenges along the way — which is even true of democracy in the United States.

What Makes Democracies Work

Since the time of Aristotle, philosophers have argued that the middle class is essential to healthy states and democracies. But what is the middle class?

In political science, the middle class refers to a measurement of social and educational standing. To illustrate this, think of a poor person with low social standing and a limited educational background who gets a new, better-paying job. From a political scientist's perspective, she would climb into the middle class. When she loses her job however, she would sink back down into poverty. Chances are, she won't be able to mobilize a political protest against her descent back into poverty because she will be too busy trying to survive each week.

Next, imagine a middle-class person with a university education struggling to find a job. Because of their continued unemployment, they sink to a lower social level. By contrast, this

---

[85] Badger, Anthony J. *The New Deal: Depression Years, 1933-40.* Macmillan International Higher Education, 1987.

[86] Hobson, Christopher. *The rise of democracy: Revolution, war and transformations in international politics since 1776.* Edinburgh University Press, 2015.

person is much more likely to engage politically and protest their slide into poverty.

Now, what would happen if the middle class grew massively, dwarfing other social classes? You would have a lot more protesting voices if anything went wrong. And that is precisely what pushed the spread of democracy — the global rise of the middle class. International studies show that middle-class people place greater value on democracy and individual freedom. They also tend to be more tolerant of alternative lifestyles than people from lower classes are. [87]

American economist William Easterly's research reveals that better rates of economic growth, education, health and civil stability are linked to a large middle class.[88] This, in turn, is tied to middle-class values of self-discipline, a strong work ethic and emphasis on long-term saving and investment. Denmark and France have their middle classes to thank for their transitions into democracy in the 19th century. Driven by their middle classes, Sweden, Germany, Britain and many other nations became fully democratized by the early 20th Century. In the Western world, the middle class has been nothing less than the bedrock of democracy.

The American Middle Class

In 1970, the top one percent of wealthy families in the United States took home nine percent of the country's Gross Domestic Product (GDP). By 2007, their share of the GDP skyrocketed to 23.5 percent. The reality is that there has been a hidden trend of decline in middle-class incomes since the 1970s. The entry of women into the workforce around that time saw an increase in average household incomes — but this masked the fact that paychecks were actually getting smaller.

Another factor masking income stagnation was the use of

---

[87] Glassman, Ronald M. *The middle class and democracy in socio-historical perspective.* Vol. 10. Brill, 1995.

[88] Easterly, William. "Happy societies: the middle class consensus and economic development." *The World Bank, Washington, DC, mimeo* (1999).

cheap, subsidized credit as a substitute for income redistribution. For politicians, this seemed like a great idea. And although a government-backed housing boom occurred as a result, it eventually culminated in the financial crisis of 2008. There is yet another factor making life difficult for the middle class and, oddly enough, it is something that benefitted them in the 19th and 20th centuries: technology.

Back then, major technological innovations created countless jobs for low-skilled workers in the coal, steel, chemical, manufacturing and construction industries. You only needed to have passed the fifth grade to get a stable job on a Henry Ford assembly line, which broke down the process of building a car into simple, repeatable steps.

While these technologies drove the rise of a large middle class and, in turn, democracy, technology today has had a rather different impact. Innovations in automation have eliminated vast amounts of low-skilled, but well-paid jobs. At the same time, new, higher-paying jobs are emerging, which reward workers with advanced skills. Back in the 19th century, math whizzes did not have too many chances to profit from their talent, but nowadays they take home much larger proportions of national wealth as software engineers, computer programmers, bankers or geneticists.

Lobbying & Government Policies

Recently, democratic institutions have become dominated by rich and powerful individuals who pursue their interests at the expense of the rest of the population. This practice is one of the most detrimental influences on American democracy and government, and is manifested in practice through lobbying, a legal form of exchanging political power for money.[89]

Although political bribery is technically illegal, gift exchange

---

[89] Campos, Nauro F., and Francesco Giovannoni. "Lobbying, corruption and political influence." *Public choice* 131, no. 1-2 (2007): 1-21.

is however permissible. The idea is that individuals that receive gifts will feel morally obliged to return the favor, and this indirect form of bribery is the basis of the entire American lobbying industry , which is not a small industry either.

Lobbying and interest groups have expanded dramatically in Washington, DC. Between 1971 and 1981, the total number of lobbying firms increased from 175 to 2,500. By 2013, the number of active lobbying firms rose to 12,000 with a combined expenditure of more than $3.2 billion to influence government policies. These lobbying firms are the ones that distort American public policy across many different areas, one of which is the tax code.

While nominal corporate tax rates in the United States are higher than most other developed nations, the amount that American corporations ultimately pay is far lower. This is because they have negotiated special exemptions and benefits for themselves through their lobbying firms.

Lobbying continues to cause a crisis of representation. The power of lobbyists and other calculating and cunning activists causes the public to feel unrepresented and voiceless. Take for instance the National Rifle Association (NRA), one of the most influential groups in Washington, which advocates for gun rights. It has an unrivaled influence on politicians and policy, and it maintains this influence at the expense of the average citizen's safety.

Conclusion

Democracy is a cornerstone of American politics. However, democratic ideals, as admirable as they are, continue to face many obstacles. The declining middle class and a crisis of representation caused by aggressive lobbying are just some of the issues that American democracy must contend with today.

10
YOUR POLITICS IS NOT MY POLITICS

Introduction

By instinct, humans are tribal creatures. That explains why teams, clubs and other types of groups inspire strong emotions among their members. We want to share our feeling of belonging with others who are like us. Tribes can be centered around any number of things. But they are not just about having something in common with others. Often, they are just as much about exclusion as they are about inclusion.

Tribes function based on two key principles. Firstly, they are based on a shared bond — ethnicity, religion, political beliefs, mutual interests or other commonalities. Secondly, tribes change the way their members think about the world. Individuals' identities often become closely linked to that of the tribe, which makes them willing to do things for the benefit of their group that they would not do as individuals.

Tribalism — the act of separating ourselves into tribes — is often overlooked when it comes to foreign policy, which is a mistake. In fact, tribalism is key to understanding how to deal with other countries. U.S. foreign policy in particular is frequently shaped by the view that nations are homogenous. Subgroups or tribes within particular countries simply are not taken into account.[90]

That is partly because America is a supergroup. It is a country made up of many tribes united by a shared national identity. American policymakers assume that other countries also have a strong bond that overrides the tribal loyalties of their citizens, but, in many cases, that is just not true. Tribal identities frequently supersede allegiance to nation-states, and as a matter of fact, foreign policies that neglect tribalism can have devastating long-term consequences.

Market Dominance

Theoretically, tribes should be able to coexist peacefully, but, in many cases, real-world power imbalances make that difficult. If one tribe is stronger than another, it is more likely than not that it might end up oppressing the weaker tribe. That in turn breeds resentment.

Market-dominant minorities — tribes that control most of a country's resources despite being minorities — are major sources of tribal tensions in many nations. Whether it is united by religion, ethnicity or something else, such a tribe's key feature is its disproportionate wealth. In Venezuela, white Venezuelans of European descent were an example of a market-dominant minority, but they were sidelined when Hugo Chávez, a representative of the country's darker-skinned majority, took power.[91]

Afghanistan provides another good example of this phenomenon. There, the small but wealthy Tajik minority was eventually overthrown by the Taliban, who were able to take power because they were backed by the country's Pashtun

---

[90] Goldsmith, Benjamin E., and Yusaku Horiuchi. "In search of soft power: Does foreign public opinion matter for US foreign policy?." *World Politics* 64, no. 3 (2012): 555-585.
[91] Chua, Amy. *Political tribes: Group instinct and the fate of nations.* Penguin Books, 2019.

majority. However, the Taliban also had powerful backers outside Afghanistan. The U.S. provided the group with weapons, which were relayed to the Islamist group by Muhammad Zia-ul-Haq, the anti-communist dictator of neighboring Pakistan. Zia-ul-Haq's agenda was far from what U.S. policymakers thought it was, however. His primary aim was not to defeat the communists in Afghanistan, rather to empower fundamentalist Islam.[92] That instance provides a great example of America failing to recognize the true ambitions of its supposed allies, and mistakenly assuming that others wanted the same things it did.

The question of what should replace a recently overthrown market-dominant minority is a tricky one. One popular option is to move away from an authoritarian government and set up democratic institutions. But this can go disastrously wrong if policymakers fail to take tribal relations into account. Navigating the transition is not easy. The market-dominant minority is understandably reluctant to give up its power. Western powers believe they are righting a wrong by helping the majority tribe take power through democratic elections. Yet, this often breeds new troubles. On the one hand, the majority might seek revenge and start oppressing the minority that used to rule over it. Then there is the minority itself. It might try to destabilize the new regime as it attempts to regain power.

The Vietnam War

Arguably, U.S. foreign policy is informed by honorable motives — Americans would like to bestow on others their values and ways of life. However, the road to hell is usually paved with good intentions, and the ignorance of local tribal politics has proved to be a major stumbling block to the effective implementation of U.S. foreign policies. The cost of these mistakes has been high, both at home and abroad.

---

[92] Williams, Brian Glyn. "Afghanistan after the Soviets: From jihad to tribalism." *Small Wars & Insurgencies* 25, no. 5-6 (2014): 924-956.

Take for instance, Vietnam. The U.S. thought the conflict within the Southeast-Asian country was between communism and capitalism. But that was not what the conflict was about. In fact, one of the aims of the Vietnamese was to liberate themselves from a market-dominant minority in the country — the Chinese. When Ho Chi Minh took power in North Vietnam, hundreds of thousands of Chinese fled southwards to escape potential persecution. The U.S. decided to throw its hat into the ring and back its supposedly "capitalist" ally in South Vietnam and actually ended up alienating their remaining Vietnamese supporters.

American involvement was hugely profitable for the Chinese minority since they controlled so much of the import and trade sectors of the economy. But the last thing the Vietnamese majority wanted was for the Chinese to become more powerful. The U.S. therefore sabotaged its own war effort by neglecting the importance of tribalism in Vietnamese history and culture.[93] If the U.S. had realized that the Vietnamese were more committed to their ethnic tribe than to capitalism, it might have pursued a different policy. By aligning itself with the majority, America would have been able to secure much greater support. As the Vietnam War ultimately showed, the willingness of people to fight for the survival of their tribe should not be underestimated.

Terrorist Organizations

Two of today's most powerful terrorist groups — al-Qaeda and ISIS — are a product of American foreign-policy miscalculations.[94] Both groups emerged because the U.S. failed to pay proper attention to political tribalism. Powerful people in tribal nations know how to leverage tribalism to advance their own agenda. Take terrorist groups for instance. They are often led by well-educated and wealthy members of tribes whose power has

---

[93] Record, Jeffrey, and W. Andrew Terrill. *Iraq and Vietnam: Differences, similarities, and insights.* DIANE Publishing, 2004.

[94] Mintz, Alex, and Carly Wayne. *The polythink syndrome: US foreign policy decisions on 9/11, Afghanistan, Iraq, Iran, Syria, and ISIS.* Stanford University Press, 2016.

been undermined in their own countries. That means they are very effective at tapping into feelings of alienation and frustration among fellow tribe members.

Al-Qaeda's Osama bin Laden, for example, was a master of political manipulation. He tried to unite different tribes into a larger group of Muslims to create a new sense of "us", which stood in opposition to "them" — the evil Americans and their allies. ISIS, on the other hand, tried to unite Sunni Muslims in a war against Shiite Muslims — a group that included Osama bin Laden's mother. That strategy allowed the group to strengthen the ties between its members while also drawing on the more general idea that the West had "humiliated" Islam. A sense of exclusion is a powerful driver of tribalism. Members of ethnic minority groups often seek out members of their own tribe. Group morality is a secondary matter; what is important is the sense of empowerment that comes with a sense of belonging.

In Western countries, the poor treatment of Muslims leaves this minority group feeling isolated. Thus, many Muslims long for an environment in which they feel respected and powerful. This creates a vicious cycle. Populist politicians target entire Muslim communities in Western countries after terrorist attacks. That in turn is likely to leave more young Muslims feeling estranged and susceptible to the sense of inclusive belonging offered by terrorist groups.

The Current Political Climate

Political tribalism has arrived in America, and it is causing unprecedented divisions in the country. Arguably, identity politics is partly to blame for this: in the U.S. today, more and more people are retreating into the comfort of their own tribes.

After the collapse of the Soviet Union, the U.S. political landscape underwent major changes. Economic questions no longer dominated politics; what became most important was the "politics of recognition", which is essentially a way of looking at oppression using the lens of race rather than that of class. That eventually morphed into today's concept of identity politics.[95]

Nowadays, the white Left sees its mission as fighting for the rights of minorities. Many would claim that is a commendable undertaking, but, for some members of society, this shift in emphasis has had an adverse effect. Many working-class whites feel that they have been left behind in their own country. That sense of disenfranchisement is what gave rise to a new tribe based on ethnicity and class.

President Trump's election can arguably be seen as the result of this change in U.S. politics. He ended up riding to power on the back of a poor majority that wanted to get rid of a market-dominant minority. The working-class majority that supported Trump believe that the American dream is no longer within their reach, but they have neither abandoned the dream itself, nor blamed richer groups, such as the wealthy capitalist owners of corporations. As they see it, the people responsible for their woes belong to a rival tribe — the coastal elite. Because the government has been in the hands of that elite for so long, they have begun to look like a kind of market-dominant minority.

At the heart of the so-called coastal elite are university-educated, cosmopolitan, middle-class Americans. They are generally left-leaning but the tribe also includes Republicans who have "lost touch" with Middle America. This hostility cuts both ways, however. Coastal elites often make fun of their fellow citizens who cling to old-fashioned ideas about what it means to be an American, and they also mock (Evangelical) Christians. In their eyes, extreme religiosity is often synonymous with backward values such as homophobia and racism.

The effect of this is to drive a wedge into American political life. Two hostile tribes have emerged. They pour scorn on each other and retreat ever deeper into their respective tribal identities.

---

[95] Lilla, Mark. *The once and future liberal: After identity politics.* Oxford University Press, 2018.

Understanding Each Other

In the U.S., an understanding of different tribes is vitally important if we want to make political progress. That is why it is both counter-productive and unfair to call Trump voters uncultured hillbillies. Thinking in those terms ends up denying millions of Americans their right to feel anxious about the way the U.S. is changing. One of such changes is in terms of life expectancy. If you are poor, white and without a high-school degree, you now belong to the only demographic whose life expectancy is decreasing.

That said, the same understanding needs to be extended to others as well. Working class whites might be worried about the future, but African Americans live in a state of real fear. They are scared that their children will be killed by the police, for no reason other than having black skin. Or that one of those anxious whites will feel empowered to "take their country back" by violently attacking minorities.

Another tribal affiliation in today's America revolves around religion. Many of the country's poorest citizens are united across race by the "prosperity gospel." Ignored by many members of the coastal elite, this religious movement supported the man who supported them — which is why some Latino and African American voters cast their votes for Trump. The prosperity gospel teaches that getting rich brings you closer to God. Because so many working-class citizens believe in the American dream and are deeply religious, it is an idea that is inherently appealing. It also speaks to them in ways that the Occupy movement didn't. To many, it felt like elites were using the plight of the working class to feel good about themselves.

Conclusion

Tribalism plays a key role in shaping political outcomes. Failure to take it into account has led to a series of foreign-policy mistakes with devastating consequences. Tribalism doesn't just affect distant countries like Afghanistan — it's also something that molds political life in the United States. But, if we want to defuse tribal tensions, we first have to understand tribes.

11
FASCISM: WHERE & WHEN?

Fascism for Power Consolidation

The word "fascism" gets thrown around quite often. On some online forums, it is used to describe police officers, in some newspaper columns, it is used to describe feminists. Some Facebook groups use it to categorize vegans or bureaucrats, and on and on. In actual fact, fascism is ideologically vague and can describe either the right or the left ends of the political spectrum.[96]

In 1920s Italy, an early hotbed of fascism, there were fascists on the left arguing for dictatorial rule in the interests of the working class, as well as fascists on the right who argued for an authoritarian government in which state and companies work closely together. In Germany, the National Socialists (Nazis) combined promises of higher pensions and better education with their anti-Semitic propaganda.

Today, governments exhibiting fascist tendencies can be found all over the ideological spectrum, from socialism in

---

[96] Poulantzas, Nicos. *Fascism and dictatorship: The Third International and the problem of fascism.* Verso Books, 2019.

Venezuela to conservative nationalism in Hungary.[97]

Invariably, the most revealing question is *not* what a fascist is. It is far more informative to ask which characteristics fascism displays. Fascism draws strength from an upset or angry public-whether that anger results from a lost war or lost territory, a loss of national pride or a loss of jobs, or any combination of these factors. The most successful fascist leaders have a charisma that enables them to connect emotionally with the crowd, converting public anger into a sense of public solidarity and purpose.

Once in power, fascists consolidate authority by controlling information. Hitler's regime went all in on the propaganda by publishing his own book, *Mein Kampf,* which was studied like the Bible. In addition, radio addresses enabled him to broadcast his hate-filled oratory to 80 million people at once. Today, authoritarian governments such as Russia and Turkey spread disinformation online and seek to quash media outlets that criticize them.[98]

A fascist normally claims to act and speak on behalf of a whole nation, or an entire group, and draws a dividing line between that group and outsiders, such as the Jews in Nazi Germany or the class traitors in Soviet Russia.

Finally, fascist leaders expect the crowd to back them up. Unlike other tyrants, they are not wary of the population and do not try to calm the crowd; rather, they strive to stir it up.

Slow is Smooth, Smooth is Fast

Mussolini, the Italian fascist dictator, once commented that one should take power as one would pluck a live chicken: as quietly as possible – one feather at a time, so to speak – so that no

---

[97] Pappas, Takis S. *Populism and liberal democracy: a comparative and theoretical analysis.* Oxford University Press, 2019.
[98] Bradshaw, Samantha, and Philip N. Howard. "The global organization of social media disinformation campaigns." *Journal of International Affairs* 71, no. 1.5 (2018): 23-32.

one notices until the job is done.[99]

Fascists rarely come to power with the suddenness of a single coup; rather, they move one slow step at a time, seeming to abide by the rules of the democratic process. This is most apparent in Hitler's rise to power, by making use of a mix of illegal and democratic means. After a failed coup in Bavaria, southern Germany, he explicitly pursued power through what he called a "policy of legality," whereby he effected electoral breakthroughs that eventually led to his appointment as chancellor. Only then did he dismantle the institutions of the state, disbanding local political assemblies, threatening political opponents, ridding the civil service of disloyal employees and establishing a totalitarian regime. [100]

Some modern-day governments also showcase how democratic means can easily be used to achieve authoritarian ends.

Recep Tayyip Erdoğan, leader of Turkey, strengthened his position step by step. After a legitimate election in 2002, he began dismantling institutions that could have provided checks and balances to his rule. Hundreds of military officers were arrested on charges – some real, some fictitious – of coup-planning. His government took ownership of unfavorable media outlets, and legislation enabled him to appoint loyal judges. Following a real coup attempt in 2016, Erdoğan instituted a state of emergency and arrested political opponents and journalists. He won a referendum giving him full authority to issue laws by decree, make arrests and deny detainees access to justice. Step by step, following his first election, Erdoğan increased his power and weakened the institutions of the state.[101]

Fascism takes hold slowly and quietly, and many people only notice it when it can no longer be hindered.

---

[99] Griffin, Roger. *Modernism and Fascism: The Sense of a Beginning under Mussolini and Hitler.* Springer, 2007.
[100] Ibid.
[101] Baser, Bahar, and Ahmet Erdi Öztürk. *Authoritarian politics in Turkey: Elections, resistance and the AKP.* Bloomsbury Publishing, 2017.

Hitler's Rise to Power

Europe in the 1920s and 1930s was a place of turmoil, especially in Germany. The country had been defeated in World War I, and in the wake of this war, many of its citizens felt humiliated. Among them was a young ex-soldier – Adolf Hitler. At one point during the war, Hitler lost his sight in a gas attack. And though he regained the use of his eyes in November 1918, the return of vision brought little relief. What he saw was a country in ruin. Germany's surrender and the victors' demands for financial reparations, as well as the country's loss of land, pained and shamed the young Hitler. He and many of his compatriots felt that Germany had been betrayed – by powerful bureaucrats, Bolsheviks, bankers and also by Jews.[102]

More than a decade later, Hitler became an incendiary political orator, but his party, the National Socialist German Workers' Party, or the Nazis, remained small. Shortly afterwards, the Great Depression hit. At the time, Germany was still paying off war reparations, by relying on loans from other countries. All of a sudden, that line of credit became unavailable. Exports markets collapsed, factory production slumped, prices skyrocketed, shops closed and unemployment surged.

Hitler exploited the panic this instilled and created an emotional connection with concerned Germans. In private, he argued that most people earnestly wanted to have faith in something and would not be too critical about what that something was, as long as it spoke to their anger, tapped into their fears and gave them a cause to rally behind.

Hitler's message, revolting as it was, delivered on those requirements. He was, he said, a simple man, standing for his country against its powerful enemies. He would fulfill the fatherland's destiny and lift his people to greatness. He delighted in how angry his speeches made his opponents, rightly seeing their indignation only encouraged his supporters. He convinced his

---

[102] Feuchtwanger, Edgar Joseph. *From Weimar to Hitler: Germany, 1918-33.* Springer, 1993.

supporters that he cared for them deeply, even when events proved that he cared nothing for their lives.

As he himself admitted, he happily told "colossal untruths," and reduced Germany's problems to a fictional but seductive single cause, saying there were "only two possibilities. Either the victory of the Aryan side or its annihilation and the victory of the Jews."

It was this rhetoric that fueled his political rise.

Fascism as a Normal Part of Human History

When we think of fascism, we tend to picture dictators such as Hitler, Mussolini and Stalin. In reality however, fascism crops up more frequently and in more places than we might think.

In the period after World War I, fascist movements were a common feature of politics. This can be seen in Britain, a country that looks back on its twentieth-century defense of freedom with pride. But it too had its own fascist movement. Sir Oswald Mosley, an eccentric Brit with a Hitler mustache, founded the British Union of Fascists on a program straight out of the fascist playbook, promising investment in public works, economic protectionism and action against foreigners, whether "Hebrew" or otherwise. Like other fascist leaders, Mosley recruited a personal security force, whose dusky uniforms gained them the name "Blackshirts," and attracted large crowds to his street rallies. It was only the shock of seeing Hitler's brownshirts invading neighboring countries that killed the acceptability of Mosley's party.[103]

Many countries witnessed similar movements. In India, Hindu nationalists concerned about Muslims in the country, and angry at British rule, sympathized with Hitler's and Mussolini's efforts to put their countries on a war footing. Elsewhere, other fascist groups emerged in Spain, Iceland, Romania,

---

[103] Dorril, Stephen. *Blackshirt: Sir Oswald Mosley and British Fascism*. Penguin/Viking, 2007.

Czechoslovakia and even in the U.S.

Fascists repeatedly come to power by promising solutions to anxiety over jobs, immigration and dissatisfactory politicians. Mussolini, for example, was successful because he understood that many Italians were frustrated with the state of their country. He advocated rejection – of the capitalists trying to exploit Italians, of the Bolsheviks trying to disrupt their society and of the status-quo politicians who talked and talked but delivered nothing. He promised to *"drenare la palude"* – to "drain the swamp" – by removing over 35,000 government officials.

Venezuela and Hungary

There are few truly fascist governments today, but many countries are proof that the line between democratic populism and fascist behavior is extremely thin.

Venezuela is one example. Hugo Chávez was elected president of the country in 1998, in a legitimate election, beating an out-of-touch government that had neglected its people. He ran on a platform to support workers and struggling families and, while in office, he used booming income from oil production to ease and improve his people's lives.

Famously charismatic, Chávez exploited his personal charm and popularity relentlessly. When he wanted to assert control over the Venezuelan oil company, he did not simply make an announcement; he invited the company's executives to join him on a live television broadcast and then fired them one by one. He personally railed against his enemies, notably the United States, in televised speeches lasting as long as nine hours.

Under Chávez, many Venezuelans enjoyed improved health care, better salaries and a renewed sense of national pride. He was no Hitler, nor was he a Mussolini, but his charisma and nationalist populism concealed the fact that he weakened the institutions of state by suspending judges, purging government officials and creating a thuggish private security force to intimidate protesters.

Following Chávez's death, Venezuela suffered under a new leader, Nicholás Maduro, who lacked both Chávez's charm and the oil riches of the 2000s. Doubling down, Maduro began rewriting the constitution and banning opposition parties.

In the heart of Europe, as in South America, other leaders are testing the limits of liberal democracy. A prime example is Hungary's Viktor Orbán. A democratically elected prime minister, Orbán has happily talked of delivering "illiberal democracy." He has relentlessly promoted ethnic pride, bemoaning the post-World War I treaty that saw Hungary lose territory and provocatively criticizing immigrants, as well as urging Magyar women – women of Hungarian ethnic descent – to have more babies. At the same time, he has used his popularity and executive power to assert control over the legal system and electoral commission.

Orbán, like Chávez was in Venezuela, may not be an outright fascist, but the warning signs are as clear as day.

Democracy's Fragility

Anyone old enough to remember the fall of the Berlin Wall will remember the sense of excitement that rose as the wall crumbled, the feeling that democracy would prevail. Today, however, that sense of excitement is receding. There is now increasing curiosity about alternatives to democracy.

The Economist's Democracy Index, which tracks democracy around the world based on indicators like respect for due process and religious liberty, recorded a decline in democracy's health in 70 countries in 2017.[104]

Meanwhile, global polls have found that while most people believe in representative democracy, one in four people thinks positively of systems that allow a leader to rule without the involvement of a parliament or a judiciary and one in five thinks favorably of military rule. How come such sentiments are on the

---

[104] Rosenthal, Alan. *The decline of representative democracy.* SAGE, 1998.

rise?

While economic circumstances today are not as terrible as in post-World War I Europe, they certainly are not ideal. In Europe, one in four young people are unemployed, with the rate higher for immigrants. Consider the successful Ph.D. student who winds up as a delivery driver or the high-school dropout who cannot find work at all; it becomes quite understandable that their faith in democratic systems might be a little bit shaken.

Technological innovation has also had an impact. Traditional professions – from bank tellers to dressmakers, journalists to taxi drivers – are being made redundant by technology. In some countries, the economic outlook is not so different from that experienced in interwar Europe 100 years ago.

Simultaneously, the same technology has disrupted trust between politicians and the public in the form of disinformation. In the American War for Independence, Benjamin Franklin used the printing press to circulate "fake news" about British atrocities.[105] Social media has however now made it easy and more or less free to distribute false information to a large audience in real time. Sitting in a coffee shop, checking the news on Facebook, it can be almost impossible to ascertain whether the source of a story is a responsible journalist, a provocateur, a foreign government or a bot.

A combination of economic uncertainty, and a lack of trust in the solutions offered by incumbent politicians, is a fertile breeding ground for fascism. All these helped bring Donald Trump into power in 2016.

Trump's Behavior and Rhetoric

The idea of the United States as a beacon of freedom, hope and democracy is ingrained in the country's history. Trump has however rejected this grand tradition, and he consistently praises

---

[105] Gorbach, Julien. "Not Your Grandpa's Hoax: A Comparative History of Fake News." *American Journalism* 35, no. 2 (2018): 236-249.

authoritarian governments around the world.[106]

Take for instance the case of Rodrigo Duterte, the president of the Philippines. Duterte is notorious for his brutal "shoot first" policy, which encourages the police and civilian vigilantes to kill suspected drug dealers. This policy has led to the deaths of more than 10,000 people, mostly in poor communities, with no due process. The volume of the killings is such that Duterte jokes that the public should invest in funeral businesses; he has also openly said that police officers on trial for abuse of power should plead guilty and he will pardon them. This was the man President Trump called and congratulated for doing an "unbelievable job."

Duterte is not an isolated example. Trump has gone out of his way to praise authoritarian leaders across the globe, from Egypt to Bahrain to Russia. For Trump, even Saddam Hussein was worthy of grudging admiration; after all, he killed terrorists without due process. Meanwhile, Trump has been quick to start arguments with America's traditional democratic allies such as Germany, Mexico and even South Korea, a country that depends on the U.S. for protection from North Korea's nuclear threats.

Trump's attacks on America's own institutions encourage anti-democratic governments abroad. His relentless criticisms of the institutions of government and modern society reach a global audience. When Trump excluded reporters representing media outlets that he disliked from a press briefing, the government of Cambodia immediately threatened to eject a group of American journalists from the country. A Cambodian spokesperson said that this was a "clear message" from the White House that these media outlets are untruthful, adding that "freedom of expression… must respect the state's power."

In China, the Communist Party has gone so far as to state that those U.S. media outlets that Trump accused of disseminating fake news can safely be ignored when they are being critical of

---

[106] Harris, Jerry, Carl Davidson, Bill Fletcher, and Paul Harris. "Trump and American fascism." *International Critical Thought* 7, no. 4 (2017): 476-492.

China and the Chinese Communist Party's policies.

The Victimhood Rhetoric

Fascist movements have always thrived on grievances: against religious and national groups, against capitalists and communists, against enemies within and outside the nation. This appeal to victimhood is familiar to anyone who has listened to Trump's rhetoric.

Trump delights in painting a bleak picture of America as a victim. During a 2017 speech in Pennsylvania, Trump complained that, for decades, the United States has suffered "the greatest jobs theft" in world history. Factories were closed, and jobs shipped away to distant countries. The United States spent "billions and billions" on global projects but failed to protect its own people when "gangs flooded into our country."

An objective critic would note that Pennsylvania's unemployment rate has decreased in recent years and that over 200,000 jobs in the state are supported through export trade. Rather, Trump's simplistic, nationalistic and pessimistic outlook is well calculated to strike a chord with people who are dissatisfied with their lot in life.

To respond to this supposed victimhood, Trump has focused on putting "America First." That is a slogan with a history, and one ill-equipped for the realities of the modern world.

In 1940, the America First Committee, composed variously of anti-war advocates and Nazi supporters, came together to fight America's involvement in World War II. The movement's popularity was given a boost by the involvement of world-famous pilot Charles Lindbergh, who openly worried that Jewish influence was pushing America toward war. Ever since, the committee, and the words "America First," has been associated with moral cowardice.[107]

---

[107] Sarles, Ruth. *A story of America first: The men and women who opposed US Intervention in World War II.* Greenwood Publishing Group, 2003.

In a modern, interdependent world, a slogan such as America First is meaningless. No challenge – whether economic or security-related – can be tackled alone. What such a slogan does, however, is signal to tyrants to do as they wish. Why shouldn't Kim Jong-un build nuclear weapons? After all, it is merely putting North Korea's interests first. Why shouldn't Vladimir Putin annex Crimea? Doing so was simply putting Russia's interests first. Trump's vision of America First legitimizes, as fascism has always legitimized, the idea that a country may do what it wants simply because it wants to.

Fascism in the United States

The United States is not currently facing fascism. President Trump may be anti-democratic, and favor authoritarian approaches to government, but, for now, democratic institutions are standing strong. It is important to bear in mind, however, that fascism creeps up on society, one step at a time.

Some Americans have argued that fascism absolutely could emerge in the U.S. – precisely because we believe it can't. The possibility of that idea is based on the fact that America's faith in its public institutions and values means people will too easily ignore their erosion, and people will hope things work out for the best until it is too late.

To avoid a splintered culture where fascism might thrive, Americans need to reconnect with each other. Present-day America is sadly disunited. A few decades ago, everyone watched the same news shows every evening, and read the same news sources – Life, Time, Rolling Stone or Newsweek. Back then, people had different views but started from a similar base of information. Today, people inhabit their own media bubbles, which reinforce, rather than counterbalance, their grievances. People are less and less willing to listen in good faith to the arguments of their political opponents.

It is not so hard to imagine an event – an economic recession, a terrorist attack or a political assassination – that could cause a decisive slide away from democracy toward fascism.

Conclusion

Fascism is not an abnormality, or an aberration, but a normal and recurring aspect of history and politics. It can be hard to detect or prevent, because it emerges slowly, and is only fully visible once in place. It thrives on grievance, division and dissatisfaction with the political status quo and is a threat to many of today's societies. It is therefore imperative to remain diligent and defend democracy whenever there are signs of it being challenged.

SOURCES

1 – Give & Take: Democratic Liberties

Agarwal, Vidhi. "Privacy and data protection laws in India." *International Journal of Liability and Scientific Enquiry* 5, no. 3-4 (2012): 205-212.

Aoki, Masahiko. "Institutions as cognitive media between strategic interactions and individual beliefs." *Journal of Economic Behavior & Organization* 79, no. 1-2 (2011): 20-34.

Gilbert, Alan, and Gilbert Alan. *Democratic individuality*. Cambridge University Press, 1990.

Lacorne, Denis. *The limits of tolerance: Enlightenment values and religious fanaticism*. Columbia University Press, 2019.

Locke, John. *Locke: Two treatises of government*. Cambridge University Press, 1967.

McGlew, James F. *Tyranny and political culture in ancient Greece*. Cornell University Press, 1996.

Mouffe, Chantal, and Paul Holdengräber. "Radical democracy: modern or postmodern?." *Social Text* 21 (1989): 31-45.

Shamsi, Rashid. "Why Islam forbids pork." *The Muslim World League Journal* (1999).

Stannard, David E. *The Puritan way of death: A study in religion, culture, and social change*. Vol. 573. Oxford University Press on Demand, 1979.

Tanenhaus, David S. "Between Dependency and Liberty: The Conundrum of Children's Rights in the Gilded Age." *Law and History Review* 23, no. 2 (2005): 351-385.

Wilson, Emily R. *The death of Socrates*. Vol. 8. Harvard University Press, 2007.

2 – Nationalism: Political Ideology or Belief System?

Brah, Aviar. "Difference, diversity, differentiation." *International Review of Sociology* 2, no. 2 (1991): 53-71.

Crossgrove, William. "The vernacularization of science, medicine, and technology in late Medieval Europe: broadening our perspectives." *Early Science and Medicine* 5, no. 1 (2000): 47-63.

Eisenstein, Elizabeth L. "The advent of printing in current historical literature: notes and comments on an elusive transformation." *The American Historical Review* 75, no. 3 (1970): 727-743.

Errington, Joseph. *Linguistics in a colonial world: A story of language, meaning, and power*. John Wiley & Sons, 2007.

Evans, Robert JW. "Joseph II and nationality in the Habsburg lands." In *Enlightened Absolutism*, pp. 209-219. Palgrave, London, 1990.

Falola, Toyin, and Emily Brownell, eds. *Landscape, environment and technology in colonial and postcolonial Africa*. Vol. 6. Routledge, 2013.

Herzog, Lisa. *Inventing the market: Smith, Hegel, and political theory*. Oxford University Press, 2013.

Horst, Steven. "Notions of intuition in the cognitive science of religion." *The Monist* 96, no. 3 (2013): 377-398.

Kalidjernih, Freddy K. "Post-Colonial Citizenship Education: A critical study of the production and reproduction of the Indonesian civic ideal." PhD diss., University of Tasmania, 2005.

Marshall, Peter. *1517: Martin Luther and the Invention of the Reformation*. Oxford University Press, 2017.

Michel, Patrick, Adam Possamai, and Bryan S. Turner, eds. *Religions, nations, and transnationalism in multiple modernities*. New York: Palgrave Macmillan, 2017.

Nugent, Walter. "Frontiers and empires in the late nineteenth century." *The Western Historical Quarterly* 20, no. 4 (1989): 393-408.

Scherer, Matthew. "Secularism." *The Encyclopedia of Political Thought* (2014): 3368-3380.

Skurativskyi, Vadym. "Mystagogue of national identification. From the notes about ethnology by Taras Shevchenko." *Філософська Думка* 1 (2014): 8-23.

Williamson, Timothy. "Necessary identity and necessary existence." In *Wittgenstein—Eine Neubewertung/Wittgenstein—Towards a Re-Evaluation*, pp. 168-175. JF Bergmann-Verlag, Munich, 1990.

3 – Ideological Racism

Benjamin, Stacy E. "Color blind? The influence of race on perception of crime severity." *The Journal of Negro Education* 58, no. 3 (1989): 442-448.

Bermanzohn, Sally Avery. "Violence, nonviolence, and the civil rights movement." *New Political Science* 22, no. 1 (2000): 31-48.

DiAngelo, Robin J. "White fragility in racial dialogues." *Inclusion in urban educational environments: Addressing issues of diversity, equity, and social justice* 2, no. 1 (2006): 213.

Gruber, Aya. "Leniency as a miscarriage of race and gender justice." *Alb. L. Rev.* 76 (2012): 1571.

Humphrey, Hubert H. *The Civil Rights Act of 1964: The passage of the law that ended racial segregation.* SUNY Press, 1997.

Kye, Samuel H. "The persistence of white flight in middle-class suburbia." *Social science research* 72 (2018): 38-52.

Lopez, Ian Haney. *White by law: The legal construction of race.* Vol. 21. NYU Press, 1997.

Montero, Darrel. *Japanese Americans: Changing patterns of ethnic affiliation over three generations.* Routledge, 2019.

Tatum, Beverly Daniel. *Assimilation blues: Black families in a White community.* Greenwood Press, 1987.

Wildsmith, Elizabeth, Myron P. Gutmann, and Brian Gratton. "Assimilation and intermarriage for US immigrant groups, 1880–1990." *The History of the Family* 8, no. 4 (2003): 563-584.

4 – True Feminism

Bair, Sarah. "The American Civil Rights Movement Reconsidered: Teaching the Role of Women." *The Social Studies* (2020): 1-9.

Blee, Kathleen. "Women in White Supremacist Movements in the Century after Women's Suffrage." *100 Years of the Nineteenth Amendment: An Appraisal of Women's Political Activism* (2017).

Delaney, Martin. *The condition, elevation, emigration, and destiny of the Colored people of the United States.* Black Classic Press, 1993.

Dobbins, Margaret Powell, and James Mulligan. "Black matriarchy: Transforming a myth of racism into a class model." *Journal of Comparative Family Studies* (1980): 195-217.

Lerner, Gerda, ed. *Black women in white America: A documentary history.* Vintage, 1992.

Meier, August, and Elliott Rudwick. "The Rise of Segregation in the Federal Bureaucracy, 1900-1930." *Phylon (1960-)* 28, no. 2 (1967): 178-184.

Meringolo, Denise D. "African American Women in the Struggle for the Vote, 1850-1920." *American Studies International* 36, no. 3 (1998): 93.

Reid, Inez Smith. *Together Black Women.* Emerson Hall Publishers, 1972.

Ruffin, Josephine St Pierre. "Address to the first national conference of colored women." *The Woman's Era* 2, no. 5 (1895): 14.

Scharrer, Erica. "More than "just the facts"?: Portrayals of masculinity in police and detective programs over time." *Howard Journal of Communications* 23, no. 1 (2012): 88-109.

Stokes, Gail. "Black woman to black man." *The Liberator, December* 17 (1968).

5 – Unconscious Biases

Czopp, Alexander M., and Margo J. Monteith. "Confronting prejudice (literally): Reactions to confrontations of racial and gender bias." *Personality and Social Psychology Bulletin* 29, no. 4 (2003): 532-544.

Greenwald, Anthony G., Brian A. Nosek, and Mahzarin R. Banaji. "Understanding and using the implicit association test: I. An improved scoring algorithm." *Journal of personality and social psychology* 85, no. 2 (2003): 197.

Hekman, David R., Stefanie K. Johnson, Maw-Der Foo, and Wei Yang. "Does diversity-valuing behavior result in diminished performance ratings for non-white and female leaders?." *Academy of Management Journal* 60, no. 2 (2017): 771-797.

Moule, Jean. "Understanding unconscious bias and unintentional racism." *Phi Delta Kappan* 90, no. 5 (2009): 320-326.

Picoult, Jodi. *Small great things: a novel.* Ballantine books, 2016.

6 – Growing Pains

Acharya, Viral V., Matthew Richardson, Stijn Van Nieuwerburgh, and Lawrence J. White. *Guaranteed to fail: Fannie Mae, Freddie Mac, and the debacle of mortgage finance.* Princeton University Press, 2011.

Bennett, Michael J. *When Dreams Came True: The GI Bill and the Making of Modern America.* Brassey's, Inc., 1313 Dolley Madison Blvd., Suite 401, McLean, VA 22101, 1996.

Eichengreen, Barry. *The political economy of the Smoot-Hawley tariff.* No. w2001. National Bureau of Economic Research, 1986.

Hornborg, Alf. *The power of the machine: Global inequalities of economy, technology, and environment.* Vol. 1. Rowman Altamira, 2001.

Iatridis, George, and Augustinos I. Dimitras. "Financial crisis and accounting quality: evidence from five European countries." *Advances in Accounting* 29, no. 1 (2013): 154-160.

Irwin, Douglas A. "The false promise of protectionism: Why Trump's trade policy could backfire." *Foreign Aff.* 96 (2017): 45.

Kehoe, Timothy J. "What can we learn from the 1998-2002 depression in Argentina?." *Great depressions of the twentieth century* (2007).

Leridon, Henri. "World population outlook: Explosion or implosion?." *Population Societies* 1 (2020): 1-4.

Liping, H. E. "China as the world's second largest economy: Qualifications and implications." *China and East Asia: After the Wall Street crisis* 33 (2013).

Peralta-Ramos, Monica. *The political economy of Argentina: power and class since 1930.* Routledge, 2019.

Rappaport, Anna, Ed Bancroft, and Lauren Okum. "The aging workforce raises new talent management issues for employers." *Journal of organizational excellence* 23, no. 1 (2003): 55-66.

Salidjanova, Nargiza. "China's new income inequality reform plan and implications for rebalancing." *US-China Economic and Security Review Commission, Washington, DC* (2013).

Salvatore, Ricardo D. "Stature decline and recovery in a food-rich export economy: Argentina 1900–1934." *Explorations in Economic History* 41, no. 3 (2004): 233-255.

Thompson, John A. "The contingent workforce: The solution to the paradoxes of the new economy." *Strategy & Leadership* 25, no. 6 (1997): 44-46.

Xi, Jinrui, and Christopher Primiano. "China's Influence in Asia: How Do Individual Perceptions Matter?." *East Asia (Piscataway, Nj)* (2020): 1.

7 – Implicit Gender Biases

Corbett, Greville G., Norman M. Fraser, and B. Unterbeck. "Default genders." *Gender in Grammar and Cognition: I. Approaches to Gender, II. Manifestations of Gender* (1999): 55-97.

Hedenstierna-Jonson, Charlotte, Anna Kjellström, Torun Zachrisson, Maja Krzewińska, Veronica Sobrado, Neil Price, Torsten Günther, Mattias Jakobsson, Anders Götherström, and Jan Storå. "A female Viking warrior confirmed by genomics." *American Journal of Physical Anthropology* 164, no. 4 (2017): 853-860.

Klafke, Raquel Forma, and Daniela Kutschat Hanns. "The Digital Evolution of Gender." In *International Conference on Human-Computer Interaction*, pp. 409-414. Springer, Cham, 2018.

Lawrence, Cera R. "On the Generation of Animals, by Aristotle." *Embryo Project Encyclopedia* (2012).

Paxton, Pamela Marie, Melanie M. Hughes, and Tiffany Barnes. *Women, politics, and power: A global perspective.* Rowman & Littlefield Publishers, 2020.

Snyder, W. S., L. R. Karhausen, G. Parry Howells, and I. H. Tipton. *Report of the task group on reference man.* Vol. 23. Oxford: Pergamon, 1975.

8 – A History of Racial Criminalization

Ackah, Yaw. "Fear of crime among an immigrant population in the Washington, DC metropolitan area." *Journal of Black Studies* 30, no. 4 (2000): 553-573.

Adachi, Jeff. "Police Militarization and the War on Citizens." *Hum. Rts.* 42 (2016): 14.

Bowling, Ben, and Coretta Phillips. "Disproportionate and discriminatory: Reviewing the evidence on police stop and search." *The Modern Law Review* 70, no. 6 (2007): 936-961.

DuPont, Robert L. "Heroin addiction treatment and crime reduction." *American Journal of Psychiatry* 128, no. 7 (1972): 856-860.

DuPont, Robert L., and Mark H. Greene. "The dynamics of a heroin addiction epidemic." *Science* 181, no. 4101 (1973): 716-722.

Ludwig, Jens, and Philip J. Cook, eds. *Evaluating gun policy: Effects on crime and violence.* Brookings Institution Press, 2004.

Miller, Richard Lawrence. *Drug warriors and their prey: From police power to police state.* Greenwood Publishing Group, 1996.

Nunn, Kenneth B. "Race, crime and the pool of surplus criminality: or why the war on drugs was a war on blacks." *J. Gender Race & Just.* 6 (2002): 381.

Roffman, Roger A. "Marijuana and its control in the late 1970's." *Contemp. Drug Probs.* 6 (1977): 533.

Rubin, Joel. "Stopping crime before it starts." *Los Angeles Times* 21 (2010).

9 – Threats to Democracy

Badger, Anthony J. *The New Deal: Depression Years, 1933-40.* Macmillan International Higher Education, 1987.

Campos, Nauro F., and Francesco Giovannoni. "Lobbying, corruption and political influence." *Public choice* 131, no. 1-2 (2007): 1-21.

Easterly, William. "Happy societies: the middle class consensus and economic development." *The World Bank, Washington, DC, mimeo* (1999).

Glassman, Ronald M. *The middle class and democracy in socio-historical perspective.* Vol. 10. Brill, 1995.

Hobson, Christopher. *The rise of democracy: Revolution, war and transformations in international politics since 1776.* Edinburgh University Press, 2015.

10 – Your Politics is not My Politics

Chua, Amy. *Political tribes: Group instinct and the fate of nations.* Penguin Books, 2019.

Goldsmith, Benjamin E., and Yusaku Horiuchi. "In search of soft power: Does foreign public opinion matter for US foreign policy?." *World Politics* 64, no. 3 (2012): 555-585.

Lilla, Mark. *The once and future liberal: After identity politics.* Oxford University Press, 2018.

Mintz, Alex, and Carly Wayne. *The polythink syndrome: US foreign policy decisions on 9/11, Afghanistan, Iraq, Iran, Syria, and ISIS.* Stanford University Press, 2016.

Record, Jeffrey, and W. Andrew Terrill. *Iraq and Vietnam: Differences, similarities, and insights.* DIANE Publishing, 2004.

Williams, Brian Glyn. "Afghanistan after the Soviets: From jihad to tribalism." *Small Wars & Insurgencies* 25, no. 5-6 (2014): 924-956.

11 – Fascism: Where & When?

Baser, Bahar, and Ahmet Erdi Öztürk. *Authoritarian politics in Turkey: Elections, resistance and the AKP.* Bloomsbury Publishing, 2017.

Bradshaw, Samantha, and Philip N. Howard. "The global organization of social media disinformation campaigns." *Journal of International Affairs* 71, no. 1.5 (2018): 23-32.

Dorril, Stephen. *Blackshirt: Sir Oswald Mosley and British Fascism.* Penguin/Viking, 2007.

Feuchtwanger, Edgar Joseph. *From Weimar to Hitler: Germany, 1918-33.* Springer, 1993.

Gorbach, Julien. "Not Your Grandpa's Hoax: A Comparative History of Fake News." *American Journalism* 35, no. 2 (2018): 236-249.

Griffin, Roger. *Modernism and Fascism: The Sense of a Beginning under Mussolini and Hitler.* Springer, 2007.

Harris, Jerry, Carl Davidson, Bill Fletcher, and Paul Harris. "Trump and American fascism." *International Critical Thought* 7, no. 4 (2017): 476-492.

Pappas, Takis S. *Populism and liberal democracy: a comparative and theoretical analysis.* Oxford University Press, 2019.

Poulantzas, Nicos. *Fascism and dictatorship: The Third International and the problem of fascism.* Verso Books, 2019.

Rosenthal, Alan. *The decline of representative democracy.* SAGE, 1998.

Sarles, Ruth. *A story of America first: The men and women who opposed US Intervention in World War II.* Greenwood Publishing Group, 2003.

ABOUT THE AUTHOR

These days, online searches have the ability to reveal a lot more information about anyone and anything than a few sentences could fully capture in a biographical paragraph at the end of a book.

I hope you found this book interesting, thought-provoking, informative, useful, educational, etc., etc.

Thank you for your time ☺